P. 28.
P. 45 ?
P. 59

P. 165

p. 138
p. 130 × 2
p. 128
p. 126
p. 125
p. 118
p. 115
p 109
p 107
p 105

The Kitchen Craft Workshop

Over 130 Quick & Easy Family Craft Projects

Ruth B. Roufberg

Illustrations by Janet Lombardo

Butterick
Publishing

COLOR PHOTOGRAPHY BY ROBIN FORBES

BOOK DESIGN BY CHRISTINE AULICINO

COVER DESIGN BY SUSAN SCHWALB

COVER PHOTOGRAPHY BY WOMETCO PHOTOGRAPHIC
SERVICES, INC.

Library of Congress Catalog Card Number 75–43281
International Standard Book Number 0–88421–024–3

Printed in USA

To Bill, Lewis, and Larry

Table of Contents

Equipment and Supplies   *133-148*

Multimedia: Drama and Music   *149-166*

Appendix *167-173*

Index *175*

Introduction

This is a different kind of craft book. Instead of the emphasis being on the finished product, the emphasis is on you and your child, how you can share the pleasure of working with your hands, and what you can learn from each other. Yes, *each other*, because parents can learn from children, as well as the other way around.

What your child will learn from you is how to use craft materials, the value of his or her own creations, and the satisfaction of seeing a project through to completion. What you will learn from your child is a free and experimental approach to materials.

And what your whole family will learn is:

• How the simplest, most inexpensive items from the kitchen can be transformed into useful and attractive objects for play, for the home, for holidays, for personal wear, and for gifts.
• An introduction to a wide variety of craft techniques:

> Assemblage
> Beadcraft
> Bookbinding
> Collage
> Construction
> Crayon resist
> Découpage
> Dyeing
> Mosaics
> Modeling
> Painting
> Paper-cutting
> Printmaking
> Rubbings
> Stitchery

Age ranges are suggested for all projects in this book. They are based on a combination of two factors: what a child of a particular age is usually able to do, and what he or she is likely to be *interested* in doing. There are a number of projects that are *easy* enough for a young child to do, but that would have no real value or use for a child, and so they are recommended for older persons.

The age recommendations are not to be taken rigidly, but simply as a guide. A seven-year-old who has had no previous exposure to art materials, or whose coordination skills are not well-developed, should start with activities recommended for preschoolers. Conversely, a child who has had a great deal of art experience, and has always shown responsibility in the use of materials, could be ready for some projects that are suggested for older children. You know your child better than anyone else; trust your judgment.

A general rule is that it is better for children to work with materials and techniques that are too simple rather than with those that are too advanced. Creativity and originality are more likely to flourish when a minimum of effort has to be expended on techniques. Even adults do their best work after they have become comfortable with their materials.

Age ranges are described in the following terms: **Preschool** means children between two and five years who are more interested in the process of experimenting and creating with craft materials than in the finished product. In the beginning they are primarily interested in the physical activity they can perform with the materials: scribbling with crayons, smearing with finger paints, crushing and tearing paper and squeezing and modeling with clay. Gradually the random activity leads to more purposeful use of materials, but even by the end of this age range, children are neither ready for, nor interested in, decorative projects or cute, novelty uses of materials.

Elementary school children are those between about six and nine years who are becoming less spontaneous and more repetitive in their creative work. In order to keep them progressing, it is important to introduce new and more stimulating materials that will encourage them to experiment. But don't provide too great a variety all at one time; that may prove more distracting than inspiring. Children are now becoming more aware of such contrasts as light and dark, rough and smooth, and spatial relationships that will help them in creating original designs for crafts.

Pre-teens are those between the ages of ten and thirteen who are developing many new skills, becoming interested in intricate details, and learning to use new tools and materials. Toward the end of this period they prefer working with friends on large projects that they cannot do alone. If you have enough space, a group of friends would enjoy making a large papier-mâché construction, a model train layout, or a play village.

Teens have just about completed major changes in their artistic development. However, there is great interest in technical skills, and this is a good time to introduce such media and techniques as mosaics, bookbinding, and jewelry-making. The final product is becoming increasingly important to teens, and they are ready to make more permanent items for their rooms, for themselves, and for gifts.

Older teens can be considered adults as far as crafts, tools, and equipment are concerned; they can work with adults on an equal level.

For a better understanding of children's artistic development from age two to adolescence, the classic book in the field is *Your Child and His Art, A Guide for Parents,* by Viktor Lowenfeld (New York: Macmillan, 1954). The author is a leading art educator who explains, in easy question-and-answer format, everything a parent could possibly want to know about children's art and creativity.

Every chapter in this book starts with basic techniques and experiments, so that both children and adults can become thoroughly familiar with each material and its possibilities. The results of these explorations and discoveries are then utilized in the projects which follow. In general, the projects within each chapter are arranged in order of increasing difficulty. Try to resist the temptation to rush into big projects before feeling comfortable with each medium.

The role of the parent is to stimulate a child's interest by introducing him or her to a variety of materials, allowing the child freedom to explore them, and giving advice only if a problem arises.

Don't show how to join two pieces of clay before the child wants to know, but do be ready to demonstrate when information is needed.

Don't give a child a pattern to trace, or a picture to copy, or someone else's original idea to reproduce. Let the child use his or her own ideas from the very beginning, making it clear that the value lies in unique methods of self-expression. As long as the child is satisfied with his or her own work, recognize that he or she is developing independence and responsibility (which will spread to other areas of life, as well).

Don't share in crafts activities by making a sample, or showing what the finished product should look like; an adult-made item looks so much better from a child's viewpoint that it may be more of an intimidation than an inspiration.

Do share by helping to set up materials and working space, and by explaining, on a shopping trip, what items are being bought for crafts and how they might be used.

Adults can also learn crafts from this book. While you are learning the techniques to show your child, you can become proficient yourself. You will learn not only *what* to do and *how* to do it, but also *why*, so that you will understand the principles and be able to adapt them to your own original work.

And that, of course, is the ultimate goal of this book: to give you enough information and guidance to dream up your own projects and bring them to fruition. It is very unlikely that you will want to make every project in this book. But each one has been tested and selected to show as wide a variety of products and techniques as possible, to help you set forth on your own.

NOTE: All products referred to in this book are described in the appendix.

Kitchen Clays:

Baker's Clay, Play Dough, Cornstarch Clay

It is especially appropriate to start this book with the various kinds of clay that can be made in the kitchen because clay is one of the first art materials a child is able to use. Watch a preschooler play with clay; there is so much that adults can learn about how to get started, and how to feel comfortable with the material.

A two-year-old will pat the clay, pound it, squish it, knead it, and try all sorts of things because he or she likes the way it feels and wants to see what will happen. In the beginning, everything is a random happening; the child pokes a finger into the clay and a hole appears. Soon comes the great discovery: "I can make a hole *whenever I want!*"

Eventually, the poking and pulling and stretching and squeezing will lead the child into shapes that seem meaningful to an adult: balls, coils, and pinch pots. An adult may exclaim in great delight over the "apples" and "snakes" and "bowls," but to the child, they are just new shapes; they don't represent anything.

Try to resist the temptation to label these shapes; if a child sees how delighted you are with what you call "apples," he is likely to try to continue pleasing you by repeating the same shapes over and over again. *You* may be pleased, but the child's creative development is being stifled. Comment on the "new thing" he has done, but don't give it a name.

Somewhere beyond the age of three, though, the child will look at a clay shape he or she has made, and there will be a spark of recognition, and the child will name the object. That's all right, because the recognition has come from within; in fact, it's another step forward. To you, it may not look like what the child says it is, but accept the label, and avoid at all costs the urge to demonstrate the "right" way to make whatever it is. Let the child's own creative and individual perception remain supreme. All too soon the unique vision of childhood will be lost.

Don't be surprised if the child occasionally goes back to formless poking and squeezing, especially after a period of being away from clay. This is often a consolidation stage before making a new advance.

Gradually, somewhere between the age of four and five, the child will take another step forward. Instead of finding a name for something *after* it is made, the child will start with an idea in mind and then proceed to form it in the clay. This is the point at which a child begins to work in a way that most adults can comprehend, with the mental plan preceding the physical representation.

Why have I described at such length how preschoolers play with clay? Because there is something for adults to learn about freedom, about experimenting, about just *playing* with the clay. For an adult who has never worked with clay, particularly with the kinds described in this chapter, I urge you not to rush into any of the projects just yet. Spend some time with your child, leisurely squeezing, poking, feeling the clay, and letting the clay dictate what should be done with it. In a period of an hour, maybe less, you will go through three years of a child's development: first experimenting, just to see what the clay can do; then finding that one of the random shapes resembles something; and finally, deliberately modeling the clay into a preconceived idea.

At that point you will be much better prepared to start one of the projects, and in fact, to make up your own projects. And that is one of the goals of this book: to give you the competence and confidence to move forward on your own and to feel secure in your ability to introduce your child to the world of crafts. You will gain personal satisfaction plus the gratification of being able to share a creative activity with your child.

The sharing can begin with the preparation of one of the three kinds of clay-like modeling materials that can be made with ingredients in your kitchen.

Baker's clay (sometimes called *bread dough clay*) is the most generally useful because it can be used by all ages, from preschoolers to adults.

Play dough is a variation of the above which is especially useful for preschoolers and young children.

Cornstarch clay is a cooked clay suitable for older children, teenagers, and adults.

Baker's Clay * * * * * * * * * *

MIX TOGETHER IN A LARGE BOWL:
- 4 CUPS FLOUR (DON'T SIFT IT; JUST SCOOP IT OUT OF THE SACK OR CANISTER AND LEVEL IT OFF)
- 1 CUP SALT

ADD, WHILE STIRRING:
- 1½ CUPS WATER, APPROXIMATELY
- 1 TABLESPOON COOKING OIL (FOR SMOOTHNESS)

Continue to stir with a fork until all water is absorbed, then squeeze the mixture in your hands to distribute the water evenly, and knead it for about 5 minutes.

Baker's clay is an uncooked clay of pleasant consistency that can be modeled into good-sized objects, and baked to permanent hardness in the oven.

In making it, note that the amount of water required is not always the same because of variations in flour absorbency due to its age, kind of wheat, and air humidity. Start with a bit less than the recipe calls for. If necessary, add a few drops of water at a time until there are no loose crumbs of flour.

At this point, a preschooler or older child can start to help by squeezing a lump about the size of a large orange. It's excellent finger exercise! Try to keep the mixture a little stiffer than seems comfortable; it will be easier to roll out and shape.

A mixer with a dough hook attachment will save time and effort for future batches of baker's clay (knead only 2–3 minutes). But let the child have at least one chance to knead it by hand.

The clay will keep a week or more in a tightly closed plastic bag in the refrigerator, but it tends to get gummy. Therefore, before using it again, bring it to room temperature, add flour, and re-knead the dough until it regains its original texture.

These are some hints and techniques that will be useful in working with baker's clay:

Keeping the clay soft. While working with part of the clay, keep the rest in a tightly closed plastic bag.

Shaping the clay. Remember that it is stronger if it is all one piece. A modeled figure is less likely to break if the head, arms, and legs are pulled out from one large oval, rather than if the head and limbs are separate pieces attached to the body.

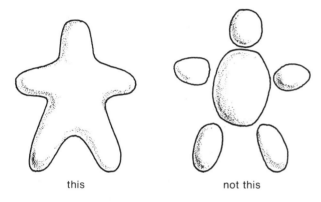

this   not this

Joinings can also be avoided by removing cutouts from a solid flat piece, rather than by joining strips.

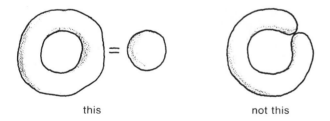

this   not this

Don't force this technique on a child. Some children see the figure as a totality and will quite instinctively pull the entire body from one piece of clay; others see the figure as a number of separate parts and will automatically attach pieces. Demonstrating the proper techniques will confuse the child and disturb the child's way of seeing things. In this case, technique can wait.

Joining pieces. If it is absolutely necessary. Moisten one edge with a wet fingertip and press both pieces together. Blend seam with the back of a fingernail, or with a toothpick or small clay-modeling tool.

Rolling. To assure an even thickness, use a rolling pin and a height guide. For a $\frac{1}{2}''$ thick circle, roll dough inside an embroidery hoop.

For a rectangle, or for a sheet of clay which will be cut into shapes, roll inside a shallow jelly roll pan that is narrower than the rolling pin. Or, tape two dowels or two pencils in parallel lines on a cookie sheet.

Coils. Roll small coils in the hands. For larger coils, slice clay in strips from a flat sheet, then roll them on a table or board with both palms. Avoid using the fingers because they cause ridges.

Thick, rounded shapes. The clay bakes most evenly when the entire object is the same thickness. If you wish to make an object which is much thicker in the middle, use a crumpled ball of aluminum foil for the center, and wrap the clay around it.

Holes. To make a hole for hanging or for decoration, use the tip of a plastic drinking straw. Just press, twist, lift up, and a circle of dough is gone! A hanging hole should be $\frac{1}{2}$ inch from the top.

Dough puffs up during baking and holes get smaller. Be sure to make the hanging hole a little larger than necessary. A hanging device that will not show from the front can be made by embedding a soda can pop-top or a bent paper clip or wire in the back of the item.

Baking. Clay needs to be baked to permanent hardness. Use a cookie sheet in a pre-heated oven. The longer the clay is baked, the harder and more durable it will be. But don't let it burn. Here are some guidelines for time and temperature:

• Oven temperature is usually 350° (never higher!) but may be lowered to 325° or even 300° for small thin items, or if a large item is browning too rapidly.

• A flat item $\frac{1}{2}$ inch thick will take about an hour to bake. Larger, thicker, or curved items need to bake longer; smaller items, less. The minimum would probably be 20 minutes in a 300° oven for a very flat, small piece such as a tree ornament or pendant.

• Look in the oven occasionally during the baking. It's all right to open the door if it doesn't have a window. If the clay is turning darker than a delicate tan, it has probably baked long enough. But if it is not yet hard (check in an inconspicuous spot or from the back with a toothpick or cake tester), lower the temperature and leave it in longer.

• Let the baked clay cool to room temperature before proceeding. For extra hardening, leave the item in the turned-off oven until it is cool.

• Interruptions in the baking won't hurt the baker's clay, so if the oven is needed for something else, it is all right to remove the clay and continue baking it later.

Finishing. Baker's clay projects need to be finished in what is usually a three-step process: undercoating, painting, and sealing. There are many products which can be used for each step, but certain sequential combinations work better than others. In most cases, the paint is selected first for its particular qualities; then compatible products are chosen to use under and over it. Appropriate combinations for felt-tip markers and fiber-tip pens, tempera paints, acrylic paint, and model airplane paints are listed in charts on page 18–19, which follow, providing some general information about the products for each step.

Basic Procedure

1. Undercoats seal the clay and provide a smooth base for paint. There is no undercoating suitable for use by preschool children. On the other hand, preschoolers don't usually care about preserving their creations, so it is unlikely that they would be baked in the first place. However, if it is desirable to save a preschooler's project, the undercoating should be done by an older child or adult.

Acrylic medium, available in art supply stores, is the best all-around sealer because it can be used by children as young as seven or eight, and all paints go over it well. Drying time is about 10 minutes.

White glue, diluted with only enough water so it can brush on smoothly, is a good substitute for acrylic medium. Drying time is about 10 minutes.

Clear nail polish has the advantage of being available everywhere. It is easy to use and it eliminates the nuisance of cleaning the brush. It can be used by children eight and older. Drying time is about 10 minutes.

Shellac is excellent; all paints except felt-tip markers go over it well. Brushes must be cleaned in denatured alcohol. Drying time is 2 hours, longer than children have patience for. Because of label cautions, shellac is recommended only for teens and adults.

Polyurethane varnish is excellent, except that it cannot be covered with either tempera paints or washable felt-tip markers. Brushes must be cleaned in either turpentine or paint thinner. Drying time is three hours. Because of label cautions, varnish is recommended only for teens and adults.

Clear plastic spray is related to polyurethane varnish. It is useful for sealing both the back and front of an object at one time, if there is a way to hang it. Because of label cautions, sprays should be used only by teens and adults.

2. Paints color and decorate the clay.

Felt-tip markers (wide tips) and **fiber-tip pens** (fine points) come in two forms: with washable ink suitable for all ages and with permanent waterproof ink which is suitable for anyone over age 8.

Tempera paints are the very best for preschoolers and young children. Colors are rich and thick, and the paint is washable, even after it has dried. The paint dries to a smooth dull finish. Tempera tends to rub off if not sealed. To give tempera a slight gloss and more permanence, mix a little acrylic medium into it for slightly older children.

Acrylic paints are the best, and most generally useful for older children, teens, and adults. Like tempera, the colors are rich and thick, but unlike tempera, acrylic paint is waterproof when dry. There is a greater variety of acrylic colors than tempera colors. The liquid paints in jars have a better consistency for painting clay than do the tube paints. Wash brushes before they dry with soap and warm water.

Model airplane paints have the advantage of being sold in small quantities at a very low price, so that a full range of colors is affordable. Clean brushes in turpentine or paint thinner. Suitable for ages 8 and up.

3. Finishes seal the paint and protect the item from deterioration. Unless there is a specific incompatibility, it is usually best to use the same product for the sealer and the finish.

Acrylic medium may be used over any paint except water-based paints, such as washable felt-tip markers and tempera paints. It makes those paints run. It *must* be used over permanent felt-tip markers because it is the only thing that *won't* cause those to bleed.

Clear nail polish may be used over any paint except model airplane paints, and permanent felt-tip markers, both of which would bleed.

Shellac and **polyurethane varnish** may be used over any paints except permanent felt-tip markers, which would bleed. Varnish is impervious to water and alcohol; shellac is damaged by both those liquids. (When not otherwise identified, "varnish" always means "polyurethane varnish.")

Clear plastic spray can be used over any paints except permanent felt-tip markers, which would bleed.

This information is put in summary form in the following charts. Select the paint first, then check the appropriate chart to determine which undercoating and which finish to use.

PRODUCTS TO USE WITH FELT-TIP MARKERS AND FIBER-TIP PENS*

	Product	Comments
Final Sealing (choose 1)	**ACRYLIC MEDIUM**	Only over permanent waterproof felt-tip pens. (Washable felt-tip pens will smear.)
	Shellac	For teens and adults only
	Varnish	For teens and adults only
	Clear plastic spray	For teens and adults only
	Clear nail polish	For age 8 and over
Paint	**FELT-TIP MARKERS** and **FIBER-TIP PENS**	Washable ink for all ages Permanent ink for age 8 and over
Undercoating (choose 1)	**NONE**	Felt-tip and fiber-tip colors are brightest directly on the clay.
	Acrylic medium	Colors will go on paler, but very smoothly.

* The products capitalized and in boldface are the best combination.

PRODUCTS TO USE WITH TEMPERA PAINTS*

	Product	Comments
Final Sealing (choose 1)	Clear plastic spray	For teens and adults
	Clear nail polish	For age 8 and up
	Shellac	For teens and adults
	Varnish	For teens and adults
Paint	Tempera	For all ages
Undercoating (choose 1)	None	For preschoolers and young children
	Acrylic medium	For age 8 and up
	White glue, diluted	For age 8 and up
	Shellac	For teens and adults

* All combinations are equally satisfactory.

PRODUCTS TO USE WITH ACRYLIC PAINTS*

	Product	Comments
Final Sealing (choose 1)	Clear nail polish	For age 8 and up
	Shellac	For teens and adults
	Varnish	For teens and adults
	ACRYLIC MEDIUM	For age 8 and up
Paint	**ACRYLIC PAINTS**	For age 8 and up
Undercoating (choose 1)	**ACRYLIC MEDIUM**	For age 8 and up
	White glue, diluted	For age 8 and up
	Clear nail polish	For age 8 and up
	Shellac	For teens and adults
	Varnish	For teens and adults

* The products capitalized and in boldface are the best combination.

	Product	Comments
Final Coat (choose 1)	Shellac	For teens and adults
	Varnish	For teens and adults
	Acrylic medium	For age 8 and up
Paint	Model airplane paints	For ages 8 and up
Undercoating (choose 1)	Acrylic medium	For age 8 and up
	White glue, diluted	For age 8 and up
	Clear nail polish	For age 8 and up
	Shellac	For teens and adults
	Varnish	For teens and adults

° All combinations are equally satisfactory.

PROJECTS

LITTLE TOYS
(Color Plate 10)

AGE: PRESCHOOL (WITH HELP) AND ELEMENTARY SCHOOL
TIME: MINUTES, PLUS BAKING AND DRYING TIME

NECESSITIES:
- Baker's clay
- Rolling pin, tray, and height gauge (see page 15)
- Wooden cocktail skewers (or alternative for axles)
- Tempera paint
- Polyurethane varnish (to be applied by adult)
- White glue

STEP-BY-STEP:

Children can usually instinctively shape whatever kind of vehicles they want; no matter how untraditional they may look to an adult, the child's version should be respected. For those who wish to make the illustrated projects:

1. Shape the vehicles.
- For cars, start with a $\frac{1}{2}$" thick rectangle, and press and pull it to form the front and rear. Cut a hole to represent windows, if desired. An adult can poke wooden cocktail skewers through the bottoms to represent axles. Fashion the wheels from flattened balls with holes pierced through the center. Bake all pieces separately, and glue them together after they are varnished.
- For boats, start with a flat oval patty. Attach two cylinders for smokestacks.
- For airplanes, pull the wings and tail from one egg-shaped piece of clay. An alternate method is to begin with two pinches of clay, one larger than the other. Roll the larger piece into a cigar shape for the fuselage; attach the smaller one crosswise for the wings.

2. Bake the vehicles in a 350° oven. The planes and boat will take about 20 minutes, the cars 45 minutes.

3. Finish the vehicles with tempera paint (no undercoat) applied by the child, and polyurethane varnish applied by an adult. This finish makes the toys outdoor as well as indoor playthings; they will not be ruined if accidentally left outdoors in the rain or in the sandbox.

JEWELRY

(Color Plates 4 and 5)

Baker's clay makes fine pendants, beads, brooches, and belt buckles. Anyone old enough to be interested in personal adornment is capable of making some form of jewelry.

Pendants and belt buckles require the same basic steps.

NECESSITIES:
- Baker's clay
- Acrylic paints and medium
- Any of the following for decorating:
  Embossing tools (gears, bottle caps, forks, etc.)
  Small seeds and beans
  Soda can pop-top rings
  Yarn, string, and ribbon
- Acrylic gel (optional)
- Pin clasp (optional)

STEP-BY-STEP:
1. Roll or press clay into a patty ¼″ thick.
2. Embellish (specifics for each are listed below).
3. Bake in 325° oven for 30 minutes.
4. Seal with acrylic medium.
5. Paint with acrylic paints.
6. Finish with a coat of acrylic medium.
7. Attach cord or yarn.

EMBOSSED PENDANT
Emboss circle with a gear, such as from a child's toy clock. Attractive impressions can also be made with a grater, meat tenderizing mallet, fork tines, soft drink bottle cap, fluted apple corer, and other kitchen or workshop items.

SEED INLAID PENDANTS
Press split peas into pendant before baking. Don't paint; merely seal with one coat of acrylic medium.

Or, set cantaloupe seeds in an overlapped pattern starting at the outer edge. (To prepare cantaloupe seeds, wash thoroughly to remove all traces of melon pulp. Spread on a tray to dry in a slow oven or in the summer sun.) Don't paint. However, because the seeds stick out so far, give them extra protection against breaking off by using acrylic gel for the final coat. Acrylic gel is a very thick white substance which acts as a glue; it thoroughly surrounds the seeds and dries to a completely clear gloss. It is highly recommended for sealing irregularly shaped attachments.

YARN DECORATED PENDANTS
Make holes with the tip of a plastic drinking straw (see techniques, page 15). After baking and painting, wrap perle cotton around pendant and continue it to become the hanging cord. Or, wrap rug yarn through pendant in an interior pattern; finish with acrylic matte varnish to avoid a shine.

POP-TOP BELT BUCKLE
Press two patties of baker's clay around an overlapping pattern of soda can pop-top rings. Start with one patty of clay, and press the rings into it in a symmetrical pattern. Top with the second patty and press both together, especially around the inserted part of the rings.

After baking, paint the center with very thick paint, stabbing the brush at it to give the rough effect of a flower head. Paint the "petals" with a cotton swab; if any bare spots show through, add a second coat of paint.

Loop a ribbon through two of the petals; tie in back.

Begin other projects in the same way but substitute a leather strip for the ribbon. Or, make it into a pendant by slipping a ribbon through only one petal. Or, make it into a brooch by pasting a pin clasp on back. The pin clasp could be inserted before baking so the pop-top flower could serve interchangeably as a brooch, pendant, or belt on different occasions!

PLAQUES
(Color Plate 3)

Plaques are of varying difficulty. The smallest ones can be made by children; the larger, more complex ones, by teens and adults.

NECESSITIES:
- Baker's clay
- Acrylic medium
- Acrylic paints
- Wood plaques, or wood or Formica panels cut to size
- Paint or fabric to cover plaques (optional)
- White glue
- Flat picture hangers (for wall plaques)

STEP-BY-STEP:

1. Form clay into desired shapes (description of each is listed below), and attach to each other, if necessary, with a dab of water.

2. Bake (see time and temperature guidelines on page 16).

3. Seal with acrylic medium, paint with acrylic paints, and finish with acrylic medium.

4. Attach pieces to background panel with white glue.

5. Hammer picture hangers into the backs (for wall plaques).

FANCIFUL ANIMALS

Children can make all sorts of realistic or imaginative animals by pressing and pulling a piece of dough into shape. They may want to make the animals they know and love best. For a snail, roll up a 4″ long coil, then pull the face and antennae from the other end. Pull a fish from an egg-shaped piece.

LITTLE GIRL

STEP-BY-STEP:

1. Take six small balls of clay. Roll one into a flat patty for the head, and lay it on a cookie sheet. Below it, place an oval patty for the body.

Add four cylinders for the arms and legs, curving the legs outward at the bottom to form feet.

2. To make the dress, first form a flat rectangle in the hands. Spread the top and bottom wider for the sleeves and the hem, while pinching in the waist.

3. Lay the shaped clay on the body; mold the sleeves, shape the collar under the chin, and flare out the skirt. Tuck the sides under the body.

The technique of attaching separate pieces, rather than pulling the shape from one piece of clay, works because the separate pieces of clay are not just laid onto the piece below, but are curved around to enclose the others, thus minimizing the possibility of separating.

4. Press clay through a garlic press to form hair, and gently arrange it around the face. (If no garlic press is available, use a smooth piece of clay for hair.)

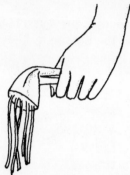

5. Add trimmings. A thin coil for the collar, flattened circle for buttons, and a shaped piece for the hair ribbon are all pressed onto the clay beneath. Pinch the eyeballs and the nose out from the face; they are so small that attached pieces would very likely fall off.

6. If desired, the arms can now be bent over the dress either to clasp hands, or to insert a ring through which dried flowers will be inserted after baking and finishing.

7. Bake and finish by following steps 2-5 at the beginning of the project.

ARTICHOKE

STEP-BY-STEP:

Because this shape and other vegetable shapes are too thick to harden thoroughly if made of solid clay, the center is a ball of crumpled aluminum foil.

1. Shape an oval patty of clay and lay it on a cookie sheet.

2. Crumple a tight wad of aluminum foil slightly smaller than the oval, and lay the foil on the clay.

3. Starting at the top of the artichoke, shape flat, tear-drop shapes and lay them, point up, on the foil. Continue overlapping leaves, making them larger as they get closer to the bottom. Curve each leaf around the ones above; press the bottoms down, but leave the tops loose.

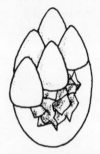

4. Just before adding the final row of leaves, roll a short cylinder for the stem. Dampen the part that will be attached to the clay.

5. Add the final row of leaves.

6. Bake in 350° oven 1 hour, or until hard.

7. When cool, coat with acrylic medium.

8. The paint is a blend of acrylic greens, blues, and yellows, with a touch of purple. Observe the real vegetable as a color guide. Children, especially, need to become aware of all the color variations in a single vegetable. First brush dark green behind the leaves and into the crevices. Blend lighter colors on the leaf surfaces, and add bits of yellow for highlights. Lightly brush purple on the uppermost tips.

9. Finish with acrylic medium. Continue with finishing procedure described in steps 4-5 at the beginning of the project.

MUSHROOM AND PEAPOD

First experiments with balls of baker's clay often resemble mushroom caps. The most logical (and easiest!) thing, then, would be to model a mushroom, or an entire plaque of mushrooms!

STEP-BY-STEP:

1. For the mushroom cap, roll a ball of clay into a sphere and flatten it out with the thumbs into a cap shape. Mushrooms come in so many variations that whatever the shape it will look like a mushroom. Lay it on the cookie sheet.

2. For the mushroom stem, make a short cylinder with an irregular bottom, and press it up into the bottom of the cap.

3. To finish the mushroom, follow directions in steps 2-5 at the beginning of the project. The paint colors for the mushroom are a mixture of white and raw umber (a dull grayish brown).

STEP-BY-STEP:

1. For the peapod, lay a curved elongated oval on the cookie sheet. Make tiny balls for peas and lay them on the center of the oval. Roll up the sides of the oval to partly cover the peas.

2. To finish the peapod, follow directions in steps 2-5 at the beginning of the project. The paint colors are a mixture of greens, yellow, and blue. Brush darker colors into the crevices, brighter green on the pod, and lighter green on the peas themselves.

ON YOUR OWN

• The methods described for the plaques can be used for a wide variety of subject matter. In addition to individual birds, animals, fruits, and vegetables, it is possible to combine and super-impose items into large plaques, such as a land-scape or harbor scene. The background can become an integral part of the plaque if it, too, is made of baker's clay.

• Ornamental wreaths are made with the same technique as the artichoke. Squeeze aluminum foil into a ring; cover it with overlapped leaf shapes cut with a cookie cutter or formed free-hand. Add any of the following:

  · Baker's clay fruits, berries, or nuts
  · Real nuts (in their shells) and pine cones embedded before baking.

If the wreath is to be painted, finish as described in steps 2-5 at the beginning of the project. If it is to remain a natural color, follow steps 10-12 under the Bread Basket project, page 26.

SEED MOSAIC PLAQUE

An 8-inch diameter plaque like this can be made by a teenager or adult. A preteen would be able to do a smaller one which would take less time and be easier to handle.

A much younger child can help by sorting seeds, selecting the nicest looking and most uniform ones. Keep a running conversation going by asking the helper to guess how many seeds it will take to complete each ring.

NECESSITIES:

• A variety of seeds, beans, or nut shells. The illustrated plaque contains:

AGE: TEENS AND ADULTS
TIME: HOURS, PLUS INTERVALS FOR BAKING AND DRYING

· White - Navy beans (also called "pea beans")
· Red - Pistachio nut shells
· Brown - Watermelon seeds (to prepare, wash thoroughly to remove all pulp, spread to dry in 325° oven for 30 minutes)
· Green - Split peas
• A plate or other circle as cutting guide, plus smaller plates, cans, or glasses for marking smaller circles
• Plastic straw to make hanging hole
• Polyurethane varnish
• Ribbon to hang

STEP-BY-STEP:

1. Roll the clay ½" thick with a rolling pin in a jelly roll pan.

2. Using a plate as a guide, cut a circle and remove the excess clay.

3. As a guide to the placement of rows of seeds, mark a series of concentric circles by lightly pressing into the clay the selected items of smaller diameter.

4. Starting in the center, press seeds, beans, or nut shells into the clay. When finished, press all the pieces again to make sure each is *in* the clay, not just lying *on* it.

5. Remove one pistachio shell from the outer row; leave the indentation because the shell will be replaced after baking. Press straw into the dough where the shell was removed, and make a hole to hang the plaque.

6. Bake in 350° oven one hour, or until hard and just barely starting to turn color. Leave in oven until cool.

7. Remove plaque from baking tray; turn it upside down over the tray and shake it to see if any loose seeds fall out. If so, paste them back on with white glue. If several of one kind have fallen out, their shapes are probably not interchangeable because of minor variations. Test to make sure each is in its proper place.

8. When glue is dry, coat the entire plaque with varnish. Tie a ribbon through the hole, then replace the removed pistachio shell with white glue. Varnish the shell and the surrounding area.

ECOLOGY BOX PLAQUE

A different arrangement of seeds can be used for a unique variation of the classic ecology box. Instead of putting the seeds behind glass in a partitioned box, embed them in areas of a clay frame.

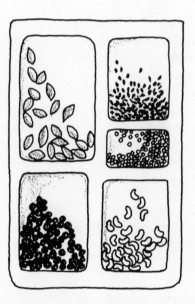

STEP-BY-STEP:

1. Roll the clay ⅜" thick and cut it into a rectangle of the desired size.

2. Cut the excess clay into strips and superimpose them around the perimeter of the plaque and on the background to divide it into different sized rectangles.

3. Press one kind of seed or nut into each rectangle. Either arrange them evenly, or bunch them into one area to look as if they had fallen into that position.

4. Make a hanging hole with a straw, and follow steps 6-8 of the instructions for the round plaque.

5. For clusters of seeds rather than a single layer, add additional layers with acrylic gel or white glue after baking but before varnishing.

BREAD BASKET

(Color Plate 7)

What could be more appropriate than a bread basket that looks like bread itself? With leftover bits of clay, bake a few "rolls" or "bread sticks" to mix in with the real ones, and see who can tell the difference!

NECESSITIES:

- 1½ recipes baker's clay
- Round ovenproof bowl or baking dish 7″ diameter or a rectangular dish. (If the perimeter exceeds 22″, additional clay will be needed.)
- Aluminum foil
- Shortening
- Cookie sheet or baking tray
- Oven gloves (optional, but useful)
- Evaporated milk and pastry brush

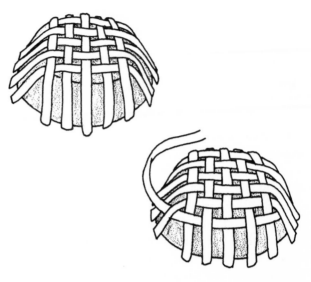

STEP-BY-STEP:

1. Turn round bowl upside down on foil-covered cookie sheet. Rub outside lightly with shortening.

2. Roll clay into ½″ thickness, 11″ long, and cut 14 strips, ½″ wide. Cut remnants into ½″ strips, too.

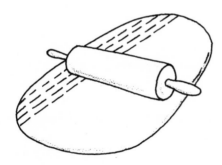

3. Roll strips into ropes, and lay five parallel ropes across the bottom of the bowl. Take five more ropes and interlace them through the first five, just like a latticework piecrust. At each intersection, dab a fingertip of water on the underneath strip and press the upper strip onto it.

4. The sides of the bowl will be woven in one continuous spiral. Take the next rope of clay and start it close to a corner intersection where it can be inconspicuously tucked between two layers of clay. Weave under and over vertical ropes, dabbing with water and pressing, just as the bottom was done. Add new rope by joining inconspicuously to the old one, wetting and pressing the ends together.

5. When the bowl is encircled once, another vertical strip is needed so the horizontal one will not go under and over the same verticals each time. Press a rope, made from one of the remnants, into place, and continue the weaving until the rim of the bowl is reached. Cut off excess ropes and dampen and press all loose ends together.

6. Put in 350° oven and bake for 30 minutes.

7. Meanwhile, roll out 3 more strips of clay 30″ long. (For easier handling, make six strips of varying lengths between 13″ and 18″ and piece them later.) Pinch rolls together with water at one end and braid the strips loosely. When piecing the strips, stagger the joinings to prevent any weak spots. Join between two layers by wetting both sides of the old and the new

roll. Leave the end of the braid separated until after placing it on the partly-baked basket.

8. After 30 minutes remove the basket from the oven, let it cool a few minutes until comfortable to the touch, then carefully move bowl and clay to a heatproof surface. Gently lift the dough off the bowl and place it back on the foil-covered cookie sheet, right side up.

9. Add the braid as the rim around the top. Wet the bottom of the braid for the first two inches and gently press it onto the rim of the clay, curving it slightly over the inside and the outside of the basket to cover the raw edges of the weaving. Continue wetting and placing the braid. Braid the end to overlap the beginning where they meet, and blend together so it looks like one continuous braid.

10. Brush braid and inside surface with evaporated milk for a nice glaze and color, and bake 1 hour more. Check every 15 minutes to be sure the weight of the braid isn't pressing down the basket unevenly. If it is, gently straighten it with oven-gloved hands.

11. At the end of the hour (or whenever the braid feels hard to the touch) turn the basket upside down again, brush the outside with

evaporated milk and bake for an additional hour. When the color begins to turn golden, lower the temperature to 300°. The longer the clay remains in the oven, the harder and more durable the basket will become. Gradually turn the temperature lower if it is coloring too fast. When it has reached the desired color, turn the oven off, and let the basket remain until it has completely cooled. If there is a pilot light in the oven, the basket can stay overnight; the warmth will harden it even more.

12. When cool, coat with polyurethane varnish. A day later, apply a second coat.

ON YOUR OWN
• Baskets can be made over different shapes of ovenproof bowls or baking dishes.
• Instead of latticework weaving, the basket can be built up with a single coil, or a twined coil made of two ropes twisted together. (Coiling is a technique used in the two classic crafts from which this project is derived: basketry and ceramics.)

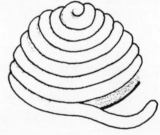

• Small bowls, for serving candy or nuts, can be molded directly on the inside or outside of gelatin molds. Roll the clay to the desired thickness, and be sure to oil the mold before draping the rolled-out baker's clay on it.

PICTURE FRAME
(*Color Plate 3*)

AGE: TEENS OR ADULTS
TIME: HOURS

NECESSITIES:
· Photographs
· 1 full recipe baker's clay (some will be left over)
· Rolling pin, tray, and height gauge
· Embossing tool (e.g. knife blade, gear)

· Cardboard
· Shellac
· Metallic airplane paint
· Rubber cement
· White glue
· Felt-textured self-adhesive contact paper

STEP-BY-STEP:

1. Select the photos to be used, and cut pieces of paper the size of the portion of each photo that is to show. (There must be a margin to extend beyond the frame opening.) Position the photos as they are to be displayed, and put the proper size paper on each photo.

2. Roll the clay ¼″ thick, using two dowels or pencils as a guide along the edge of a cookie sheet. Lay the papers on the clay as the pictures are to be arranged, and cut away openings that size. Leave at least a 1″ margin between photos and around the outside edge.

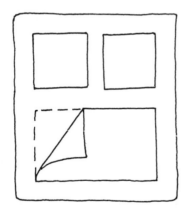

3. Emboss a design on the frame. The center can be incised with a knife blade, and the edging can be beveled by rolling a gear all around the outside at an angle.

4. Bake at 325° about 45 minutes. In order to keep this piece from stretching out of shape, bake it on the same pan on which it was rolled, rather than lifting and moving it to another baking surface. This gives it a tendency to stick, so after five minutes in the oven, when the shape is beginning to harden but is still soft enough not to have stuck, remove the pan from the oven and slide a spatula under the clay to make sure it is loosened from the pan.

5. Baker's clay has a tendency to develop air holes and to puff up in unwanted places, like an unfilled piecrust. Since it is essential for the frame to be perfectly flat, it is necessary to check it every five or ten minutes. If it has puffed up anywhere, remove it from the oven, and puncture the air hole with a cake tester or a needle inserted from an inconspicuous angle. Also, gently press the frame down with the spatula, then return the pan to the oven.

6. When hard, remove from oven and let cool. Lay another cookie sheet on top to keep it flat while cooling.

7. Use a shellac undercoat, metallic model airplane paint, and a final coat of shellac.

8. Cut cardboard ½″ smaller than the outside dimensions of the frame. Lay the frame on it and draw a pencil outline of the openings. Remove the frame, and attach the pictures with rubber cement where indicated.

9. Spread white glue on the back of the frame and paste it onto the cardboard. Hold in place for several minutes, then let dry for at least 30 minutes.

10. Cover the back with felt-textured contact paper cut ¼″ smaller than frame. Display on easel.

ON YOUR OWN

• Color the dough while preparing it by adding food colorings, beet juice, or grape juice to the water.

• Color the dough while preparing it by adding mustard powder, paprika, or turmeric to the dry ingredients.

• Shape the clay in a small mold, such as individual fluted tart shells, for candle holders. Bake a metal screw-top from a bottle into the top of each mold, to hold the candles.

• Make a Christmas wreath by braiding three ropes of clay (or twisting two ropes) into a circle. Insert walnut shells, peanut shells, and pine cones between the coils. Leave spaces where sprigs of holly and other greenery can be inserted after baking.

Play Dough * * * * * * * * * * *

> MIX:
> - 2 CUPS FLOUR
> - 1 CUP SALT
>
> ADD:
> - ½ CUP WATER
>
> SQUEEZE TO MIX.
> TO RETARD SPOILAGE DURING STORAGE, ADD:
> - 1 TABLESPOON VINEGAR
> - ENOUGH TALCUM POWDER TO IMPROVE THE SMELL.

This is ideal for a preschooler or young child for the following reasons:

• He or she can have the satisfaction of making it all alone (if the ingredients—a measuring cup, and a large bowl—are set out), and thereby be more highly motivated to play with it.
• There's an unobtrusive arithmetic lesson in measuring the ingredients.
• There's good finger exercise in mixing and coloring the dough.
• The clay is coarse-textured and suitable for the gross manipulations of a beginner.
• The clay is not to be baked, so there is no pressure on a child to "make something pretty."
• The process of mixing the clay leads right into the process of playing with it, which tends to lengthen a child's attention span.

A child will start by just squeezing and patting and kneading and poking the dough to see what will happen; there's no interest yet in making anything, and this should not be forced. It is just an experimental learning stage. If the adult is also a beginner at clay, he or she could play right along with the child.

When the child's interest palls, or at the next play session, introduce color. Ask the child to hold the clay over a bowl and make a thumb hole in it. Put a few drops of food coloring into the hole and let the child mix it. The first few squeezes will marbleize the dough, an intriguing phenomenon. It takes considerable additional squeezing to blend the color smoothly. One color at a time is enough for a two-year-old to use, although an older child might enjoy separating the dough into several parts, making each part a different color.

At the end of the play time, store the clay in a plastic bag in the refrigerator. (Put a label "CLAY" on it, partly so no one mistakes it for something to eat, but mainly to introduce to a young child the concept of names, writing, and reading.)

Cornstarch Clay * * * * * * *

> STIR TOGETHER IN A SAUCEPAN:
> * 2 CUPS BAKING SODA (A 1-POUND BOX)
> * 1 CUP CORNSTARCH
>
> ADD ALL AT ONCE:
> * 1½ CUPS COLD WATER
>
> The mixture is very sticky and lumpy at first. Stir slowly until it becomes thin and smooth. Then cook over medium heat while stirring constantly, until the mixture thickens to the consistency of mashed potatoes. When it is no longer shiny and is too thick to stir any more, turn the mixture out onto a plate or cookie sheet, and cover it with a damp cloth until it is cool.
>
> Then, knead it like dough and form it into the desired shapes, or store it in a tightly closed plastic bag in the refrigerator until ready to use. It keeps well for a week or more.

Cornstarch clay is prepared by cooking the ingredients, and the making of it should therefore be limited to teens or adults, although pre-teens will also enjoy using it.

The clay is extremely fine-textured and particularly suitable for small, thin objects that are preplanned and precisely shaped. (By contrast the baker's clay puffs up during baking, thus obliterating fine details.)

Both the preparation and the use of cornstarch clay make it incompatible with the needs of very young children.

These are techniques for working with cornstarch clay:

Coloring. The clay itself can be colored before working with it, or the finished article can be painted afterwards.

If the entire batch is to be the same color, add food coloring to the water during the preparation.

Otherwise, tint it afterwards. For several colors, divide the cooled clay into portions and mix a different food coloring into each.

To avoid stains on the hands, squirt the food coloring into a thumb hole made in the middle of the clay, and try to contain the color within the clay for as long as possible while turning and folding the outside to the inside. Blue seems to stain the fingers the most, and children should be encouraged to use other colors.

The color will lighten a lot as the clay dries, so be sure to add enough food coloring to make an extremely intense shade.

For coloring finished items, the very same paints appropriate for baker's clay can be used on cornstarch clay. (See paints, page 17.)

Shaping. Cornstarch clay can be shaped in any of these ways:

* *Model it* with fingers or in the hands.
* *Roll it* between two pieces of wax paper with a rolling pin, and cut shapes with a knife, cookie cutter, or other shaped cutting devices.
* *Push it* through a cookie press.

Drying. Depending on the size of the object, clay will harden at room temperature in one or two days. To hasten drying, preheat the oven to 350°, then turn off the oven and put in the clay, on a baking sheet or a cardboard box. Clay can also stay overnight in an oven with a pilot light.

Regardless of the method, be sure to turn the clay over occasionally so that all surfaces are exposed to the air.

Pasting. Build complex forms by pasting slab-shaped pieces together. This is similar to the slab method of building used in ceramics. Rub the edges to be joined with medium-fine sandpaper (e.g., #120) to remove surface irregularities and assure a tight fit. Join with white glue; press together for a few moments, then let set for 30 minutes.

Painting and finishing. The same products and combinations of products listed for baker's clay are suitable for painting and finishing cornstarch clay. However, the cornstarch clay is extremely absorbent, and it takes three or four coats of shellac or varnish to get a good gloss. Acrylic medium does the job in only two coats, and because of the shorter drying time, it is generally more satisfactory.

PROJECTS

PENDANTS
(*Color Plate 4*)

AGE: PRE-TEENS AND UP
TIME: MINUTES TO HOURS, WITH IN-
TERVALS FOR DRYING

Pendants are a good project for getting the feel of the clay and experimenting with all the previously listed techniques for coloring, shaping, drying, and finishing.

NECESSITIES:
  · Cornstarch clay
  · Rolling pin, tray, and wax paper
  · Cookie cutters
  · Incising tools (e.g. knife blade, gears, kitchen gadgets)
  · Toothpicks
  · White glue
  · Yarn
  · Varied paints and finishes

STEP-BY-STEP:
  1. Roll cornstarch clay ⅜″ thick and cut with cookie cutters between 1½–2″ diameter.
  2. Decorate and finish as desired, or follow directions below for pendants.
  3. To hang a pendant high at the throat, leave hanging cords open at the ends for tying. This means the center of the yarn must be looped through the hole in one of the following ways.

Note that one method shows two vertical strands, and the other shows one horizontal.

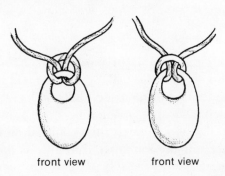

front view   front view

4. For a low-hanging pendant that can slip over the head, the knot can be concealed. Tie the ends first, then loop the yarn as in step 3, positioning the knot behind the hole. Secure the knot in place with a dab of white glue.

STAR-SHAPED PENDANT
Make indentations across the front with a knife blade. Pierce a hanging hole by rotating a toothpick. Let dry, and paint with permanent felt-tip markers, adding two coats of acrylic medium. Loop yarn hanging cord through the hole. Color

the yarn with a felt-tip pen to match the clay underneath.

ORANGE-BORDERED PENDANT

Press a piece of yarn into the clay with a knife blade and continue it to become the hanging cord. Paint with washable felt-tip markers and dip twice into a can of polyurethane varnish. Let varnish dry between dippings.

FOUR-POINTED PENDANT

Simply paint with permanent felt-tip pens. This hanging hole goes from side to side. Make by inserting a toothpick which stays in during the entire drying process and rotate it occasionally to prevent sticking. Coat the pendant with two coats of acrylic medium.

METALLIC PENDANT

Incise with a kitchen gadget that simultaneously cores an apple and sections it into wedges. Paint sections with model airplane paints in metallic gold, silver, and copper. Drip India ink into the incised lines. Give the pendant two coats of acrylic medium. (For less gloss, acrylic matte varnish may be used.)

ON YOUR OWN

• Pendants can be made three-dimensional by pasting smaller shapes on top of the base—for instance, a series of concentric circles.
• Some of the same techniques used with baker's clay pendants would be appropriate: embossing with textured objects, cutting out interior areas, and embedding seeds or stones.
• See also the instructions for making a mirror in the section on miniature furniture (page 35–36); the technique could be used for making a pendant containing a photo of someone special.

BEADS

(*Color Plate 5*)

AGE: PRE-TEENS AND UP
TIME: MINUTES TO HOURS, PLUS DRYING TIME

Don't decide on any one style of beads before playing around with different shapes. The illustrations will provide a start, but there will be much more satisfaction in waiting for an original inspiration.

NECESSITIES:
· Cornstarch clay, pre-colored with liquid food coloring
· Rolling pin, wax paper, and tray
· Small round cutter (e.g., apple corer)
· Toothpicks
· Acrylic gloss medium
· Plasticene (plastic clay) or alternative substance for inserting toothpicks (see step 3)

STEP-BY-STEP:
1. Shape small pieces of clay as desired, or follow instructions below for illustrated beads.

2. Rest the beads on a flat surface to harden. Turn them occasionally so all sides are exposed to the air.

3. Finish beads with two coats of acrylic gloss medium, allowing drying time between coats. To coat entire bead at once, push the bead onto a toothpick inserted into a column of plasticene, as illustrated.

4. String finished beads on plastic-coated wire, dental floss, perle cotton, or (if the holes are large enough) yarn.

DISKS

Roll clay to $\frac{1}{4}''$ and cut circles with a fluted apple corer. (As an alternative, a doughnut hole cutter or jar cap could be used.) Twirl a toothpick in the center to make a hole.

MARBLEIZED CYLINDERS

Combine leftover bits of clay from other projects. Squeeze them together just enough to marbleize the colors. Roll the clay with the palms into a long roll, then slice into $\frac{1}{2}''$ sections. Reshape the sections if they have become flattened during slicing. Insert a toothpick in the center, and twirl it occasionally so the clay doesn't harden onto it.

TWISTED DANGLES

Take a pinch each of three separate colors of clay and shape between the fingers into three small rolls. Lay them next to each other, press together slightly, and twist. Insert a toothpick at one end, and turn it occasionally to prevent the clay from hardening onto it.

TEARDROP TWISTS

Make a short roll of clay and flatten it slightly. Twist the ends, then bring them together and press flat. Insert toothpick as described above.

COLLAR NECKLACE

(*Color Plate 5*)

AGE: TEENS AND ADULTS
TIME: HOURS, PLUS INTERVAL FOR DRYING.

A necklace that looks like a collar can be made of rolled clay, cut into wedge-shaped plaques. This project requires precise work.

NECESSITIES:

· 1 recipe cornstarch clay
· Wax paper
· Rolling pin
· Ruler
· Knife
· Toothpicks
· Permanent waterproof fiber-tip pen (or alternative paint)
· Acrylic medium
· Plastic-coated wire (or alternative stringing cord)

STEP-BY-STEP:

1. Roll clay to $\frac{1}{4}''$ thickness. Cut tiles 2" long, and tapering from 1" at the bottom edge to $\frac{1}{4}''$ at the neck edge. Here's how to mark the slab of clay.

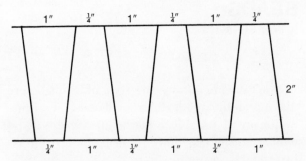

2. The necklace requires 14 tiles, but cut at least 20 to allow for experiments with designs, paints, and finishes—and possible mishaps.

3. Also cut between 16 and 20 small tiles to duplicate the upper $\frac{5}{8}''$ of the large tiles.

4. Insert a round toothpick through each tile

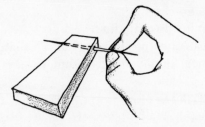

crosswise, about $\frac{1}{4}''$ from the top, and twirl it around. Twist occasionally while the tiles are drying, and then remove toothpicks. Turn the tiles occasionally during drying so all surfaces are exposed to air.

5. If there are any shape irregularities in the dry tiles, smooth them out with sandpaper. Start with medium-fine (#120) and finish with fine (#220).

6. Paint design on tiles with permanent waterproof fiber-tip pens. (For alternative paints, see suggestions under techniques for painting and finishing, page 17.)

7. Apply two coats of acrylic medium, or appropriate finish for the paint selected. A low lustre finish is more attractive than a high gloss. First do the backs and the surrounding part of the sides and let dry; next, do the fronts and the surrounding part of the sides and let dry. Repeat,

allowing half a day drying time for the second coat.

8. String onto plastic-coated wire of a color to match the design, or use one of the alternatives suggested in the section on beads.

ON YOUR OWN
• An alternative way of cutting these tiles would be based on a circle. Make an inner circle whose circumference equals that of the neck. Draw an outer circle 2″ beyond. Slice the wedges as if being cut from the center of the circle.
• Cut tiles in other shapes.
• Alternate long and short tiles.
• Try other designs. Tiles could be made to look like dominoes. Or long white tiles and short black ones could be arranged to look like a piano keyboard.

MINIATURE FURNITURE
(*Color Plate 1*)

AGE: PRE-TEENS AND TEENS
TIME: HOURS TO DAYS, WITH INTERVALS
FOR DRYING

Flat pieces of clay can be glued into three-dimensional objects, such as miniature furniture. This bedroom uses only about one-third of a full recipe of cornstarch clay, but it's necessary to have extra for rolling and cutting, so make a full recipe. There will be enough left over for a few more rooms of furniture.

All the pieces of furniture must be visualized as separate tops, sides, fronts, and backs to be joined. The fitting-together must be figured out in advance, and it will be an interesting challenge to those who have a good perception of spatial relationships. Children may need the help of an older person who has built models from scale drawings.

To duplicate the furniture shown in the photograph on page 33, refer to the scale drawing

for the shapes of pieces to be cut out. The scale is $\frac{1}{4}'' = 1$ foot. For furniture to be used in a miniature playhouse the child already has, use the same scale as the house.

NECESSITIES:
· 1 recipe cornstarch clay
· Food coloring
· Graph paper for planning shapes to cut
· Cookie sheet or other flat smooth surface for rolling clay
· $\frac{1}{4}''$ dowels to tape to sides of cookie sheet for height gauge
· Rolling pin and wax paper
· Ruler, preferably transparent dressmaker's ruler marked in $\frac{1}{8}''$ grids, for transferring accurate measurements to clay

· Knife, preferably a short-handled knife with a sharp but not pointed blade. Such a knife will be easy to cut with and will also be used for flattening and reshaping edges which have become distorted during cutting. An artist's palette knife is ideal; otherwise, a cocktail knife or canape-spreader.
· Baking tray or cardboard for drying pieces
· White glue, for joining pieces
· Acrylic medium

STEP-BY-STEP:

1. Prepare the clay. Make one recipe cornstarch clay. Set aside a piece the size of an egg yolk for the white pillow case and sheets. Divide the rest in half. Color one part with 10 drops of red food coloring, and the other half with 12 drops of blue food coloring. The color will lighten tremendously as the clay dries, so don't hesitate to use even more food coloring if the color doesn't seem sufficiently intense.

NOTE: If a window is to be made, look ahead to that section now because the sky must be made while the blue clay is being mixed (page 36).

2. Make the furniture.

CHAIR

Roll pink to $\frac{1}{4}''$ thickness. Cut out chair parts. Set aside to dry, keeping parts in same relative position to indicate where the joinings are to be made. When dry, paste seat to sides and backrest, following instructions under pasting tech-

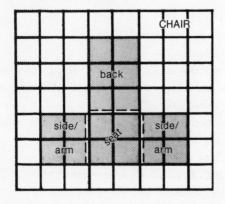

niques on page 29. When glue is dry, model cushion, armrests, and backrest by hand, press onto the frame, and let dry.

BED

This bed was formed over a child's wooden block ($\frac{5}{8}'' \times 1\frac{3}{8}'' \times 2\frac{3}{4}''$). A very close approximation is the top of an individual-serving cereal box. Cut the box $\frac{5}{8}''$ below the top, and use the top as the base to be covered. Pat the white clay as thin as possible, and put some of it at one end of the base to represent the sheet. Roll the pink, left from the chair, even thinner; add a narrow strip of white at one end to represent the folded-over top sheet. Cut the clay, and drape the blanket and sheet over the bed. Pinch the corners.

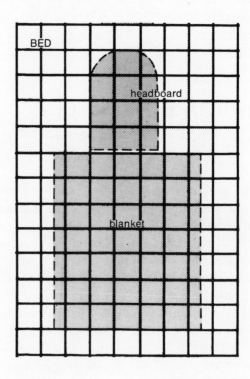

PILLOW

Model the pillow by hand. For a realistic effect, pinch corners to a point.

HEADBOARD

Roll blue clay ¼″ thick and cut headboard according to pattern. Let headboard, pillow, and blanket-covered bed all dry separately. When hard, glue together.

BEDSIDE TABLE

Roll clay ¼″ thick. Cut top as indicated on pattern. For the base, roll a cylinder by hand to ½″ diameter, then cut it to stand ¼″ high. Let both parts dry separately; when hard, glue together.

DRESSER

Roll blue clay ¼″ thick and cut pieces according to pattern. Note that the back and front are narrower than the top. This is to compensate for the thickness of the sides. The furniture will be glued together like this:

Compensating for the thickness in planning and glueing is important so furniture looks like this. (Remember this when designing original furniture!)

Use a knife blade to incise the design of drawers on the dresser front. Make toothpick indentations to represent drawer pulls. Let all parts dry separately; when dry, glue together.

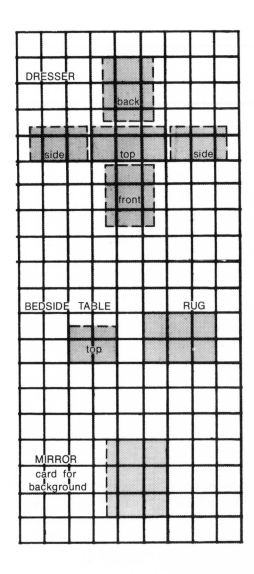

MIRROR

Cut a file card, or similarly stiff paper, ¼″ narrower than the dresser and the desired height. Wrap aluminum foil (shiny side out) around it tightly, and smooth out the front with a finger-nail. Lay the "mirror" on a piece of clay, and cut around it, leaving a ⅛″ margin. Remove excess clay, cut away tiny triangles at the corners, and fold the rest of the margin up and over the "mirror" like a frame so that the mirror cannot fall out. (A "painting" can be similarly done; paste a magazine picture on a card backing, and proceed as for mirror. Do the same for the picture on a TV set.)

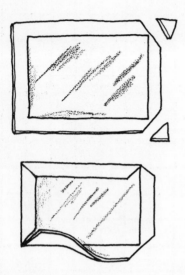

WINDOW

While mixing the blue clay, when it becomes nicely marbleized to look like a gently cloudy sky, roll out the clay and cut what will look like the view through the window. Let that piece start to harden while mixing the rest of the blue to an even color and while making all the rest of the furniture. By then, the "sky" will have hardened sufficiently to add the curtains.

Cut two pink strips, each half the width of the window. Flatten them between the palms and drape them over the window. Tie-backs may be added. A ruffled top piece will conceal unevenness at the upper edge; be sure to press it into the layers below.

RUG

For a striped rug, lay strips of two colors next to each other. First push them together with the fingertips to make sure they stick; then roll a rolling pin or the side of a jar over the rug to flatten it. Make fringe by incising with knife tip.

ACCESSORIES

Adorable miniatures, like the flowerpot, book, slippers, comb, and brush, can be made with tiny bits of clay, a toothpick, and imagination. For the hairbrush, cut off a tuft of bristles from an old toothbrush. Holding the tuft firmly between your fingers, wrap clay around one end.

3. Finish the furniture.

Seal the furniture and accessories with two coats of acrylic gloss medium, allowing drying time between coats. For a more realistic dull finish, the blanket and the sky may be coated with matte varnish instead.

ON YOUR OWN

• Make furniture for other rooms. Build miniatures for other hobbies: an airport with planes and a control tower; a space station with rockets, space capsules, and robots; a marina with boats; a service station with cars and gas pumps; model ships and model cars.

• Everything can be made white, and painted after the parts are assembled. This would permit such options as plaid or printed upholstery and curtains.

FLOWER PLAQUE MOSAICS
(Color Plate 3)

Teenagers can make the mosaic pieces (tesserae), but even pre-teens will enjoy embedding them, particularly if the pieces are not too tiny.

NECESSITIES:
- 1 recipe cornstarch clay
- Food coloring
- Acrylic medium
- Long-bladed knife or spatula
- Paper plate and other bases for mosaic backgrounds
- Tile grout (optional)

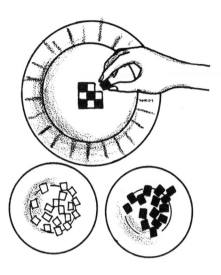

STEP-BY-STEP:

1. Set aside ⅓ of the white clay to be used as background (if tile grout is not used). Divide the remainder into as many portions as necessary and color each with a different food coloring. The clay will lighten a lot as it dries, so make the colors exceedingly dark to provide a good contrast between the colors and the white background.

2. Roll each color clay separately to ⅛″ thickness. Remove it from the rolling surface and transfer it to another surface, to prevent sticking. With knife, incise a grid pattern in squares between ⅛″ and ¼″. Try not to cut all the way through because that will tend to distort the squares. Cut *nearly* all the way; then, the tiles can be snapped apart after they are dry. Around the edges where there is no more room for squares, cut some triangles, rectangles, and irregular shapes; don't let any of the uneven edges go to waste. Let harden overnight.

3. Separate the pieces and put each color in a separate tray or plate.

4. Roll out the white clay ¼″ thick to fit into the flat center part of a 7″ diameter paper plate. Push the colored pieces into the clay, starting from the center and working in all directions towards the outside. The flower design is done free-form; if a preplanned design is being copied, transfer it to the background clay by making slight indentations with a knife.

5. When finished, press all the pieces down again, to make sure they are embedded. Let harden, preferably in the oven with only the pilot light on.

6. After about half a day the plaque will be hard enough to be loosened from the plate. Turn the plaque over so the back can harden.

7. When the back is hard, glue it back into the paper plate, and apply two coats of acrylic medium to the front.

8. Make a hole in the rim with a hole-puncher, and hang on a ribbon.

ON YOUR OWN

- For glazed tiles and a dull background, coat the tiles before breaking them apart. Embed them in instant tile grout, which is available in hardware stores and ready to use right from the can. It is not a product for young children to use, however.

- Use leftover tiles to make paperweights. Cut the bottom from a styrofoam cup; it should be ¼″ deep. Spread tile grout evenly with a knife to the level of the rim. Press pre-coated tiles in, and let dry. Jar lids could also be used as a base for paperweights.

• Color the background clay or tile grout; then some of the tiles to be embedded can remain white.

• To transfer a pictorial design to mosaics, rule off the design in square grids, and transfer the pattern to background clay by selecting the appropriate color tile for each square.

Papier-Mâché: Pulp and Strips

Papier-mâché is French for "chewed paper." The French pronunciation is "pop-YAY-muh-SHAY," which may give rise to children's calling it "mushy paper." However, we have Anglicized the first word and we pronounce it just like "paper."

Papier-mâché is very likely the most versatile craft medium ever discovered. It makes lightweight, but extremely durable, objects ranging in size from tiny beads to large furniture. The thing that holds it all together is a simple flour-and-water paste!

There are two forms of papier-mâché:

• *Pulp* is shredded paper mixed with paste to the consistency of clay ("poor man's pottery," it has been called), and it is modeled like clay. Most of the preparation should be done by teens or adults, although children as young as three or four will enjoy tearing the paper.

• *Paper strips* are torn and pasted in multiple layers to cover a pre-formed foundation. Young children can use this method of papier-mâché, but some of them might not have the patience to tear the necessary uniform size strips, so it might be better for an adult or an older child to prepare a supply of strips beforehand.

How does one decide when to use pulp and when to use strips?

Pulp is better for:
· Teens and adults
· Complex shapes, such as the model train landscape (page 53–54) and puppet heads (page 156)

· Covering another object when you want to alter the shape, such as the bracelet (page 57) and the pencil holder (page 45)
· Situations where the rough texture will enhance the design
· A modeling approach, in which you shape the object in your hands, with or without the help of tools

Strips are better for:

· Children
· Simple shapes like spheres, cylinders, and flat surfaces
· Covering another object without changing the basic shape
· Situations where a smooth finish will look best
· An architectural approach, where you cover a prepared shape (even though you may have made the shape yourself)
· Decorations that are based on the color or pattern of the paper itself

In some cases, either method can be used. It is a good idea for a beginner to try both methods, as suggested in the first projects; perhaps you will have a strong preference for one method or the other.

Pulp takes longer to prepare than strips. But strips take longer to apply. And both take a day or longer to dry, and as much additional time to paint and finish. Papier-mâché is thus a rather slow medium, best for people who have patience and don't expect instant results.

But the good news is that you don't have to

spend a great deal of time *all at once* on papier-mâché. You can do one step today, wait several days or a week until doing the next stage, and so on. In fact, papier-mâché is better if allowed to dry more than thoroughly between steps, so it may be just the thing for you if you have only short periods at a time to spend on it.

What can be made from papier-mâché? There are four ways to use papier-mâché; the first three are adaptable to either pulp or strips.

• Cover an existing object that would otherwise be discarded, such as a weather-beaten patio table, a cracked plate, caterers' trays, and other white elephants.

• Use an existing object as a mold, such as a balloon for making a mask or hat, or a bowl to make duplicates.

• Make your own inner structure (armature) on which to build a landscape, animals, or other sculptures.

• Model an object freehand entirely from pulp.

All four methods are included among the projects which follow.

Pulp * * * * * * * * * * * * * * * *

There's no getting around the fact that it takes time to make papier-mâché pulp. But it's easy and can be done in stages.

NECESSITIES:
- Newspapers
- 6- or 8-quart kettle
- Blender (optional, but highly desirable)
- Strainer (about 5″ diameter)
- Bowl
- Old cloth (about 8–10″ square)
- Plastic storage container with cover

STEP-BY-STEP:
(These instructions call for newspapers, although the same procedure can be used for softer paper such as paper towels, toilet tissue, or paper napkins when a finer-textured pulp for more advanced or detailed work is desired.)

1. Tear the newspaper sheets into quarters along the folds (or into halves, if it's a tabloid newspaper). Tear one sheet first horizontally, then vertically, to establish the "grain line" —

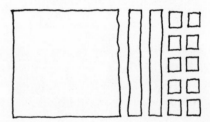

that is the direction in which it tears straighter. Then tear all the sheets into strips along the grain about 1″ wide, and then crosswise at 1″ intervals.

Smaller is better but, lacking sufficient time or patience, 2″ lengths will do. Make enough to pack a 1-quart measuring cup three times — or more in order to be ready for a second batch of pulp.

2. At night bring to a boil a 6- or 8-quart kettle half full of water, and sprinkle the three tightly packed quarts of papers into it. The sprinkling is essential. If papers become wet while they are stacked together, they will become matted like cardboard and will impede the pulping procedure. Sprinkle them in a few at a time, letting each layer get wet before adding the next layer.

Cover the kettle and let the water boil until bedtime; then turn off the heat and let the papers soak overnight.

3. The next morning, let the paper and water boil again until about two hours before working with it. (It takes time for it to cool enough to handle.) If it cooked for a while the night before, more cooking really isn't necessary.

4. The easiest way to convert the papers into pulp is in a blender; however, be aware that a plastic carafe and base will become stained from the printing ink and will have to be scoured.

Put about 1 cup of papers and 2 cups of water into the blender and turn it on. If it is a variable-speed blender, start it at low and gradually turn it to high. The wet papers are very heavy, and unless a high proportion of water is included, the paper may either pack the blades so they cannot spin smoothly, or may stay suspended above the whirling blades. If either of these things happens, add more water.

To pulp the papers by hand, take a handful at a time and scrub them together either between the fingers or through a strainer. Wear protective gloves to keep the printing ink off hands.

5. Empty the contents of the blender into a strainer over a bowl and press out as much water as possible with a metal spoon, or by hand. Turn the remaining pulp in the strainer into a square of cloth (an old sheet or T-shirt) and twist the

cloth around it to squeeze out the remaining water. This step is also done with hand-pulped paper. It is important that the pulp be as dry as

possible so it can absorb the maximum amount of paste later. Repeat with the rest of the newspapers.

At this point, the pulped newspapers can be stored in a tightly covered plastic container for up to a week.

6. Make paste. There are several kinds of pastes used with papier-mâché. For this method use thick paste.

THICK PASTE
- 1 CUP FLOUR
- ENOUGH COLD WATER TO MAKE A SMOOTH PASTE
- 2 CUPS BOILING WATER
- 2 TBSP. WHITE GLUE

Pour the cold water/flour mixture into the boiling water and stir for about five minutes until it becomes exceedingly thick and smooth. Remove from heat, stir in white glue, and let the mixture cool to handling temperature. At this point, the paste can be refrigerated for up to a week in a covered jar; it will get thicker and lumpier, but will retain its effectiveness.

7. Wait until starting a project before mixing the pulp and the paste. The neatest way is in a plastic bag. Put any quantity of pulp in a plastic bag, together with half as much thick paste. Squeeze and knead until the white paste no longer shows. At this point the paste will not yet be thoroughly blended, but the mixture will not be too sticky to handle. Remove it from the bag and squeeze a handful at a time through the fingers until there are no more lumps. Add more paste to reduce the size and number of lumps. Continue adding as much more paste as the pulp can absorb, but don't let it get too wet, or it might develop cracks during drying. All together, it should be possible to work in about three-fourths as much paste as pulp. Remember, the more paste, the better it will stick together.

Pulp which has dried out can be restored by soaking in hot water for about 5 minutes. Squeeze water out, and mix in additional thick paste.

These techniques are used in working with pulp:

Applying pulp. There are three main methods for applying pulp.

• *Press* it on with the fingers, a pinch at a time. This method gives the greatest texture, and was used for the pencil holder (page 45) and for the trees in the model train landscape (page 54).

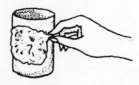

• *Roll* it with a rolling pin between two sheets of wax paper, then lift it up and wrap it around an object, as for the bowl (page 48–49) and the mountain tunnel in the model train landscape (page 53–54).

• *Model* it in the hand in one lump, just like clay, as for the puppet head (page 156).

Incising a design. To create an incised design, make indentations in the wet pulp with a knife blade, bottle cap, or any sharp object. These indentations can either be the final decoration, or can mark the place where cord will later be glued.

Drying. The best way to dry papier mâché pulp is outdoors on a sunny summer day. (Or days . . . pulp is slow-drying.) Otherwise, any warm place, such as in front of a warm air vent, will do. But don't put it into the oven because drying too quickly can cause the pulp to shrink too fast and crack. Also, keep it in a dry place; too much humidity can cause it to turn moldy before it finishes drying.

Depending on its size and thickness, papier-mâché pulp can take anywhere from overnight to several days to dry thoroughly. Drying starts from the outside and proceeds inward, so even when the surface feels dry, it may not be dry through and through. It is far better to let it dry longer than necessary than to paint and finish it too soon.

Finishing. The order for the finishing steps (some optional) is:

1. If desired for smoothness, spackle (available in hardware stores) may be applied, or the surface may be sandpapered.

2. If string decorations are to be glued on, do that now.

3. Seal the surface of the pulp with a coat of acrylic gesso and let it dry.

4. Paint with tempera or acrylic paints and let dry.

5. Glue trimmings, if desired.

6. Apply clear finish (acrylic varnish, polyurethane varnish, clear plastic spray, epoxy resin).

There is a commercial product known as instant papier-mâché available in art, hobby, and craft stores. It is a dried pulp-and-paste mixture which requires only the addition of water and a few minutes of kneading to be ready for use. But it takes just as long as homemade pulp to dry and finish. There may come a time for using the purchased product, but as long as a child is being introduced to crafts, it's certainly nice to do as much from scratch as possible. And much cheaper!

Strips ✳ ✳ ✳ ✳ ✳ ✳ ✳ ✳ ✳ ✳ ✳ ✳ ✳ ✳ ✳

The basic papier-mâché strips are the long grain-line strips torn exactly as in Step 1 of the instructions for pulp. If the newspaper texture or pattern will be an integral part of the design, make uniform strips by tearing the papers against the side of a ruler. If the newspapers are merely for underlayers for strength, the strips may be torn freehand.

For very small areas or curved ones, it may be necessary to tear the strips into shorter lengths, but don't take the time to do this until the need arises. During an evening of TV-watching, fill a supermarket bag with enough paper strips for quite a few projects. These techniques are used in working with strips:

Applying strips. There are two ways in which strips can be applied.

Dipping. Strips are dipped into paste, and the excess is removed by pulling the strips between two fingers. The strips are then laid smoothly

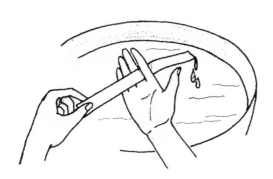

on the object to be covered. This is a slow-drying method which is good for children who work slowly, or for situations in which it may be necessary to alter the shape while working, such as forming an animal.

The dipping paste is *thin paste*.

> THIN PASTE
> Mix
> · ¼ CUP FLOUR INTO 1 CUP WATER.
> Stir into 3 cups boiling water. Boil and stir for 2–3 minutes. Let it stand until cool enough to touch. This paste can be saved for up to a week in the refrigerator, but it will turn rancid at room temperature.

Pasting. Strips of paper, either wet or dry, are applied onto the object to be covered, and each layer is brushed with paste as soon as completed. This method is neater than dipping because the hands don't have to touch the paste; however, children may have difficulty in brushing on the paste without disturbing the placement of the strips, and for children, this method lacks the immediacy of getting into the paste. The dry strip method is the quickest to do and the quickest to dry.

The paste for this technique is a *medium thick paste*.

> MEDIUM THICK PASTE
> Mix
> · ½ CUP FLOUR INTO 2 CUPS OF COLD WATER
> in a saucepan. Stir until completely smooth. Bring to a boil over a medium flame, then lower the flame and stir constantly until thickened and bubbling.

This paste can also be made in double quantity, and stored in the refrigerator for up to a week.

Layering. Add layers by one of these methods in order to be sure each layer completely covers the preceding one.

• Apply each layer of strips perpendicularly to the previous layer.

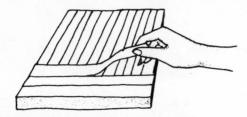

• Use different, easily identifiable papers for alternate layers; e.g., every other layer can be colored comics or classified ads or stock market pages. (For this method, it would save time to sort the papers before tearing them, and to store them separately.)

If the surface is getting too wet (especially for dipped strips), apply a layer of dry strips.

For extra strength, insert a layer of fabric strips dipped in liquid starch.

Binding. This technique is used to give a smooth and strong finish to any object with corners or edges. It is done with short paper strips folded over the sharp edge, each overlapping the previous strip halfway. If the binding goes around to the starting place again, it is good to lift the first strip and lap it over the last to make a completely smooth finish. Binding can be done several times during the building up of the article, as well as for the essential final step.

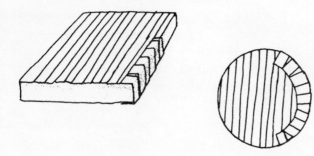

Final layer of strips. The final layer of strips may require special consideration if the papers themselves are to form the design of the finished item:

• For smoothness, the final layer should consist of small torn rectangles rather than long strips.
• For texture, the final layer could be cardboard cut-outs, cord, or nylon-reinforced paper towels.
• If the newsprint is to show, select an appropriate part of the paper, such as TV listings for an evening snack tray, supermarket ads for canisters.
• The final layer can be gift wrap paper, magazine pictures, other decorative papers, or even fabric to correlate with the decor of a room.

Drying. Drying strips is the same as for pulp, except that objects that can fit into the oven may be put there with just the pilot light on.

Sealing. Sealing is necessary if the papers already applied do not constitute the final design. Seal the surface with a coat of acrylic gesso. For additional smoothness, three or four additional coats of gesso may be applied, each brushed in a different direction. Rub with sandpaper between coats.

Decorating. Methods depend on the maker's age and the subsequent use of the project. Young children like to simply paint their papier-mâché with tempera in a very spontaneous way. Older children tend to have a more definite idea of the effect they want, and they may do some preplanning of color schemes on scrap paper. In any case, tempera is the best decorating medium for children. When they have a need for something more sophisticated, they will ask; meantime, let them exhaust the possibilities of tempera, and don't suggest anything else before they are ready.

Decorative finishes for teens and adults include:

· Acrylic paints
· Colored tissue papers, applied with either acrylic gloss medium or white glue diluted with only enough water to make it brush on smoothly. Colors show up especially well when applied over a white surface (gesso or several layers of white tissue paper). Papers may be torn or cut, crumpled or smooth,

overlapped or in a single layer, according to the effect wanted. Experiments may be done on white posterboard or on a gessoed carton. If the colored tissue papers appear too garish, use a final single layer of white tissue.

- For high relief, glue on any of the following:
  - Cardboard shapes, which may then be painted (tiny pieces could form a simulated mosaic)
  - Colored cord or twisted tissue paper curved in elaborated scrolls
  - Tissue paper crumpled, drenched in white glue, and applied to the surface
  - Upholstery fringe for the edge of a table or a tray

In the beginning, it is best to use only one decorative finish; later, a variety of papers, fabrics, and other embellishments can be combined.

Finishing. Any of the following finishes may be used:

- Acrylic medium
- Shellac or varnish (shellac dries faster)
- Spray varnish, if the shape is too complex to brush
- Epoxy resin for bowls or dishes which will be washed in hot water and detergent

PROJECTS

COVERING AN OBJECT WITH PULP

PENCIL HOLDER
(*Color Plate 6*)

AGE: ELEMENTARY SCHOOL AND UP
TIME: HOURS, PLUS DAY OR MORE FOR
      DRYING

(Younger children may need help with the simulated pencil, or they may want to omit it entirely.)

NECESSITIES:

- A can, metal or plastic
- Papier-mâché pulp
- A skewer or thin dowel
- Sandpaper
- Tempera paint
- White glue
- Yarn or string
- Varnish
- Clear plastic spray

STEP-BY-STEP:

1. Apply pinches of pulp to the outside of the can. Sometimes pulp will not adhere to plastic; in that case, wrap masking tape around the container first.

2. Stick a bamboo skewer, dowel, or other stiff support halfway into the pulp, half exposed. Cover the exposed part with pulp and shape to a point at the top.

3. When thoroughly dry, use sandpaper to smooth the shape of the point.

4. Paint with tempera, and let dry.

5. Write the owner's name by squeezing a thin stream of white glue on the pencil holder. Press yarn or string onto the glue and let dry.

6. An adult should do the rest:
   a. Spray with clear plastic and let dry.
   b. Brush varnish on the outside of the pencil for a realistic gloss, and on the yarn to add stiffness.

ON YOUR OWN

• Other appendages and other painting can be added to cans.

• Cover a cup, and make the handle into a nose. Cover a sugar bowl and make the handles into ears. These are good ways to recycle cracked or chipped dinnerware.

• For a slightly smoother application, the pulp could be rolled and wrapped around the container. Smooth with a knife blade, as if buttering bread; repeat later when the pulp is partly dry and the texture has roughened again.

• Pins stuck into dry pulp make an excellent substitute for a cork bulletin board. Roll pulp in a jelly roll pan or other frame. To hang it without a frame, push holes into it with a dowel while still wet. Paint as desired, although the natural pulp color looks quite appropriate.

COVERING AN OBJECT WITH STRIPS

STRIPED CONTAINER
(*Color Plate 6*)

AGE: ELEMENTARY SCHOOL AND UP
TIME: MINUTES, PLUS DAYS FOR DRYING

Containers can be covered with paper strips also, and if the final layer is a decorated paper, such as a combination of marbleized and solid construction paper, the decoration is completed during the construction. A project like this is something a young child can manage easily, but don't expect as uniform a design. Young children don't preplan designs, and the end result will be more of a random collage arrangement which will have a charm of its own. Control the results somewhat by providing only a limited choice of papers.

NECESSITIES:
· Cylindrical salt or cereal box
· Newspaper strips
· Thin dipping paste in a bowl
· Strips of construction paper
· Shellac

STEP-BY-STEP:

1. An adult should cut the top of the cylindrical box to the desired height.

2. Apply strips by the dipping method to the inside and outside of the container. Layers should go in alternate directions as described in techniques for strips. Across the bottom, they should be arranged like spokes. When the surface gets too wet, apply one layer of dry strips.

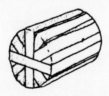 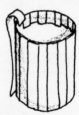

3. For the final layer, use torn strips or squares of construction paper, bringing them over the top towards the inside.

4. Let dry. This will take a long time because damp papers are applied to both sides of absorbent cardboard. Plan on leaving it for a week.

5. When dry, an adult should shellac it. (Varnish may also be used but it causes irregular mottling on some construction papers; test it first.)

ON YOUR OWN
• Trays may be covered with strips. Use shabby ones on hand, plastic ones from the 5 & 10, or caterers' trays.
• Make a set of canisters from 1-lb., 2-lb., and 3-lb. coffee cans. Use epoxy resin finish so they will be washable.

REDECORATED TABLE
(Color Plate 7)

AGE: ADULTS
TIME: DAYS

This is a renovation project for beat-up furniture, such as a patio table with rusted wrought iron legs and a peeling tile top.

If the metal is in good condition, it could simply be repainted. If not, papier mâché leads to a complete rejuvenation.

NECESSITIES:
· Half-sheets of newspaper
· Newspaper strips
· Cellophane or masking tape
· Medium thick paste
· Old sheet or other tight-woven fabric
· Liquid starch
· Acrylic gesso
· Sandpaper
· Upholstery fringe
· Colored tissue paper
· Acrylic gloss medium
· Epoxy resin finish

STEP-BY-STEP:
1. Cover the legs with tubes of newspaper made by rolling three half-sheets together. Tape. Cover with four layers of pasted strips applied in a spiral; alternate the direction of each layer.

2. The fastest way to build up a large flat surface is with pasted layers; both the top and bottom of the table are done this way. Cut a pattern for the top to allow for the sides to be folded down. Cut ten sheets of newspaper to match the pattern, and layer them together, with coats of paste between the sheets. Put this aside while preparing the paper for the underside of the table.

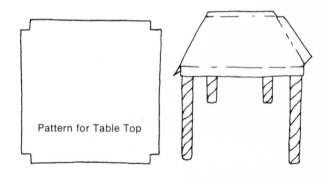

Pattern for Table Top

3. Trim the pattern to fit the underside of the table. This will mean cutting off the flaps, as well as cutting indentations where the legs

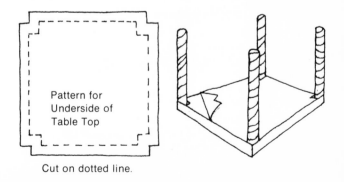

Pattern for Underside of Table Top

Cut on dotted line.

are. Make a ten-layered piece, as above, and paste it in place.

4. Paste the layered sheets on top, folding the sides down to cover the sides of the table. Let the entire table dry.

5. For extra strength and stiffness, cover all surfaces with fabric dipped into liquid starch. The necessary pieces are:
- Rectangles to wrap around legs
- Two pieces for top and underside, the same as the layered sheet patterns
- A long strip to wrap around the perimeter of the tabletop

6. Cover the wet starched fabric with a layer of dry strips, and let the entire thing dry; Then add three more layers of pasted strips and let dry.

7. Brush on a coat of gesso; when dry, go over it with fine sandpaper.

8. Glue upholstery fringe around the edge of the tabletop, and gesso it into place with a second coat of gesso applied to the table in the opposite direction from the first.

9. At this point, the table could be painted monochrome or in any pattern. Or it could be left white and varnished. In the example shown in Color Plate 7, the top was patterned in a design of colored tissue papers applied with acrylic gloss medium. The legs were painted to match one of the colors.

10. Coat the entire table with epoxy resin finish to make it waterproof.

ON YOUR OWN
- Make snack trays from foil containers for frozen food entrees. Use epoxy resin finish so they will be washable.
- Make a handbag from a man's lunch pail or a child's lunch box.
- Cover 6-pack cartons from bottles (not cans) of soft drinks or beer. Use one as a server for cold drinks; another as a tip-proof holder for children's paint jars.
- Rigid objects don't need multiple layers of paper strips, unless the shape needs to be altered. Coffee cans, for instance, would need several layers in order to conceal the indentations; other kinds of cans might not.
- The final layer need not be decorated paper or construction paper. The plain newspaper strips can be sealed with gesso. A young child, particularly, will then enjoy painting it however he or she likes. Or if the containers are going to be used for toy storage, it would be nice to paste a picture of what is to be kept in it, e.g., crayons, checkers, dominoes, etc. (Then print the *word* beneath the illustration so the child will associate the written name with the object.)

PULP WITH A MOLD

PAINTED SNACK BOWL
(*Color Plate 7*)
AGE: TEENS AND ADULTS
TIME: HOURS, PLUS DAYS FOR DRYING

NECESSITIES:
- A bowl to use as a mold
- A coating for the bowl so the pulp can be easily removed. One of the following:
  - Petroleum jelly
  - Cornstarch
  - Aluminum foil or plastic wrap (wrinkles will transfer to the pulp)
- Papier-mâché pulp
- Rolling pin
- Wax paper
- Knife
- Spackling compound (optional)
- Acrylic gesso
- Acrylic paint
- Acrylic gloss medium or epoxy finish

1. Roll out a circle of papier-mâché pulp, larger than the bowl, between two sheets of wax paper. Lift up the pulp and place it on the coated bowl. With the palms of the hands, gently press the flat pulp to the curve of the bowl. Use a knife to cut away the excess and to smooth out the cut edge.

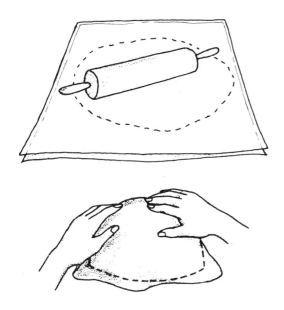

2. For extra strength around the rim, press some of the cut-away pulp around the edge to make a thicker lip. (Also save some of the pulp for Step 3.) Blend it into the existing pulp with the back of a fingernail or other smooth object. For greater, all-over smoothness, slide a knife blade over the surface of the pulp as if buttering bread. Repeat when the pulp is partly dry because the texture tends to roughen up again as the moisture evaporates.

3. When the outer surface is dry, gently lift the pulp off the bowl and turn it right side up so the inner surface can dry. (If petroleum jelly has been used, it will have to be removed with alcohol after the inside of the bowl is dry.) The depression formed by the foot rim of the bowl should be filled in at this time with leftover pulp and smoothed out. Let dry completely.

4. To smooth the rim, use sandpaper. To smooth the inner surface, spread with spackling compound, which is available at hardware stores. If a rough-textured surface is preferred, skip this step.

5. Seal the bowl with a coat of acrylic gesso (or two, for additional smoothness). Paint with acrylic paints and finish with acrylic gloss medium. An alternate finish, so the bowl will be washable, is epoxy resin finish.

ON YOUR OWN

• Using an appropriate size tray as a mold, make a set of snack trays. After unmolding each one, a raised ring of pulp can be added in one corner of each tray to hold a glass or cup.

STRIPS WITH A MOLD

FIREMAN'S HAT
(*Color Plate 11*)

AGE: ELEMENTARY SCHOOL AND UP
TIME: HOURS, PLUS DAY OR MORE FOR
      DRYING

Start with a couple of children's play hats to get the technique; then go on to a sunhat or other sporty headwear.

NECESSITIES:
- A round balloon
- Bowl into which the inflated balloon will fit snugly
- Crayon or felt-tip marker
- Newspaper strips, about 1″ wide and 12″ long
- 10 quarter-sheets of untorn newspaper
- Bowl of paste
  (thin paste for dipping, page 43, if a child is going to participate; otherwise, medium paste, page 43)
- Cornstarch (optional)

- Acrylic gesso
- Red tempera paint
- Polyurethane varnish
- Small piece of cardboard
- Aluminum foil
- White glue

STEP-BY-STEP:

1. Inflate a balloon to a circumference about $\frac{1}{2}''$ larger than the child's head. (The extra allows for the possibility of some air loss in the balloon; if that doesn't happen, the size can later be decreased by adding strips to the inside.

2. Draw a line around the "equator" of the balloon with a crayon or felt-tip marker.

3. Place the balloon, knot down, in bowl. Coat the upper part with one of the following to enable the papers to be easily removed later:

- Two layers of overlapping strips of wet paper (with *no* paste). This takes longer than the next alternative, but is failproof.
- A liberal patting of cornstarch.

4. Apply strips of paper by either the dipping or pasting method (page 43). Do ten layers for dipping, or eight for pasting, then let it start to dry.

5. When the outside is firm, but before it is rock hard, slip it off the mold and press the edges gently to conform to the shape of the head. It comes off the balloon completely round, but most heads are wider behind the temples, so the crown will have to be eased into an oval shape. For complete accuracy, a fitting is recommended.

6. Let the entire crown of the hat dry, inside and out. The shape may be held with the aid of rubber bands or by wedging the hat between heavy objects.

7. When dry, add binding strips (page 44). If the crown is not rock hard, add half as many layers of strips as previously, by the same method, and another row of binding. When dry, try on the hat for size in order to determine which method to use for attaching the brim: on the outside if the size is right; on the inside if it is large.

8. To prepare the brim, lay the crown on a stack of ten sheets of paper, and trace around the crown. Also draw the oval shape of the outside of the brim of a fireman's hat. Cut through all layers of paper, cutting an inner circle $\frac{3}{4}''$ smaller than the crown shape, and cutting the outer edge on the line.

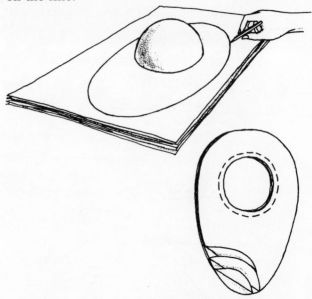

9. Stack the ten layers with layers of paste in between. (Place the crayon-marked sheet somewhere in the middle; the gesso later used may not cover it well.) While still damp, cut slits an inch apart from the center to the marked line. Turn up the flaps and paste them onto the crown of the hat, either inside the crown or outside, depending on whether or not the crown needs to be made smaller.

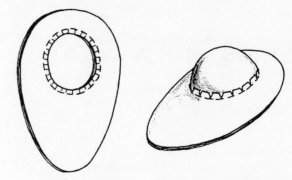

10. Paste two layers of strips (one perpendicular, one horizontal) over the seam both inside and out, and bind the outer edge of the brim.

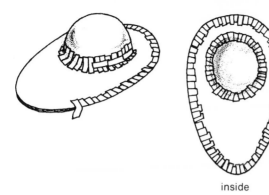

inside

11. When dry, seal with gesso. Paint with red tempera. (Even if an adult has done everything up to this point, the child who is going to use the hat should be given a chance to paint it.)

12. An adult should varnish the dry hat with polyurethane varnish. This is waterproof, and a suitable outdoor finish so the hat may be worn even in the rain.

13. A child can make a badge from cardboard covered with aluminum foil. Attach it to the hat with white glue.

ON YOUR OWN

Construction Worker's Hat. Make a narrow brim which can be curved upwards while still damp. Paint it yellow.

Police Officer's Hat. Use just a half-brim. The high shaping in front can be added with a crushed paper armature after the crown is removed from the balloon mold, and before adding the extra strips for hardening.

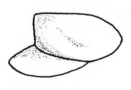

Coolie Sunhat for teens or adults. Make a 10-layer circle, slit a radius, and overlap the cut edges until the size fits. Cut away the excess, and join the cut edges with extra layers of pasted strips.

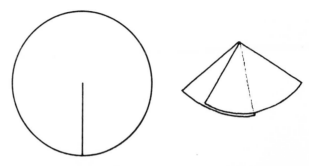

High-crowned Hat for teens and adults. Cut a strip whose length equals the head circumference, a circle the same size for the top, and a brim with the same size inner measurement. In this case, the attaching flaps are on both edges of the straight-sided piece, rather than on the top and brim. A rippled brim, may be shaped while the layers are still damp.

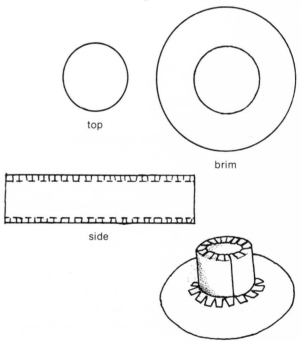

top

brim

side

Puffy Beret for teens or adults. Construct by adding crumpled newspaper to the balloon before starting to paste the strips.

Masks. The lengthwise half of an oval balloon can also be used as a mold for masks. Or cover a balloon completely, and cut off the hardened paper in two lengthwise halves, making two masks. Eye, nose, and mouth holes can be cut afterward, or can be allowed for in advance by attaching empty thread spools or bottle caps where the paper strips should not cover.

STRIPS WITH A MOLD

PAPER CUT-OUT SNACK BOWL
(*Color Plate 7*)

AGE: TEENS AND ADULTS
TIME: HOURS, PLUS A DAY OR MORE
       DRYING TIME

NECESSITIES:
  · A bowl to use as a mold
  · Newspaper strips
  · Medium thick paste (page 43)
  · Acrylic gesso
  · Sandpaper (#320 or #400)
  · Acrylic paints
  · Origami paper (optional)
  · Rubber cement
  · Epoxy resin finish

STEP-BY-STEP:
1. The inside of the bowl is used as the mold. If the outside had been used (as in the snack bowl made with pulp), there would have been a depression where the foot rim was. With pulp it is easy to fill in the area; with paper strips it is not. Putting the strips inside the bowl will give a smoother inner surface.

However, the outside (bottom) will also be perfectly smooth, which is not good. A foot rim is necessary to prevent the bowl from wobbling. It can be made without adding attachments. Start with two layers of plain wet strips (with no paste), arranged in overlapping spokes. So many layers cross over the center that it effectively makes a concave bottom on the bowl.

2. To compensate for the irregular shape inside, some of the subsequent layers are not crossed over the center. Two patterns for applying such layers are illustrated below:

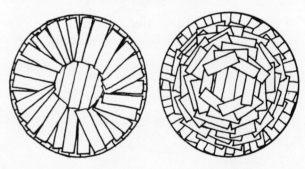

3. Apply a total of six full layers of pasted strips. When dry:
  · Remove from the mold
  · Cut the outer curve where necessary to even it
  · Bind the edges
  · Add three more layers of strips inside and outside to further stiffen it and refine the shape
  · Finish with a final row of binding strips

4. Apply three or more coats of gesso on each side, using fine sandpaper between coats after

the second. Use as many coats as necessary to make the finish sufficiently smooth and white.

5. Paint and decorate the inside and outside. The illustrated bowl was painted on the outside. The inside has a design cut from origami paper, a very thin paper which comes in richly colored squares. It is sold in art, stationery, and hobby shops, and in stores which sell Japanese goods. The technique for cutting it is a refinement of the snowflakes we all made in kindergarten. Fold the paper in half diagonally two or three times. Cut away small shapes along the fold lines. Open up the paper, and admire the pattern produced by the repetition of negative spaces. The cut-aways may be added to embellish and enlarge the design.

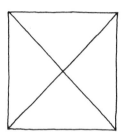 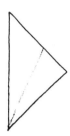 

Cut along outlines.

For a curved bowl, one point is essential. *The edge of the paper must be cut into; otherwide the paper will not be able to curve to the contour of the bowl.*

Wrong. This paper can only stay flat.

Right. The corners of this paper will be able to curve upward.

6. Attach paper design with rubber cement. (White glue causes paper to wrinkle; rubber cement prevents this.) When dry, spray with clear plastic to set the paper. To make the bowl washable, give it a final coat of epoxy resin finish.

ARMATURE COVERED WITH PULP

MODEL TRAIN LANDSCAPE
(Color Plate 10)

AGE: TEENS AND ADULTS, WITH PAR-
TICIPATION BY YOUNGER CHILDREN
TIME: HOURS, SPREAD OVER SEVERAL DAYS

This project is planned for HO gauge, which has a scale of 1:87. In round figures, $\frac{1}{8}''$ represents one foot.

NECESSITIES:
- One full recipe of papier-mâché pulp
- Chicken wire and wire clippers for armature (alternatives: round cereal box or twisted newspapers)
- Rolling pin
- Wax paper
- Tissue paper (blue, green, yellow)
- Acrylic gloss medium
- Acrylic matte varnish
- Acrylic paints
- Stones, pebbles, or gravel (optional)
- White glue
- Toothpicks

STEP-BY-STEP:

1. Make an armature to support the pulp. The one illustrated was made from a piece of chicken wire 19″ x 8″ bent into a tunnel shape with two flat extensions on the sides.

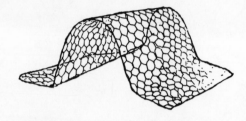

2. Add a curve of chicken wire at the tunnel opening and on one side to simulate a more massive mountain.

3. Optionally, the armature could be made from a round cereal box with one side, the top and bottom cut away; or from newspapers twisted into shape and held with masking tape and string.

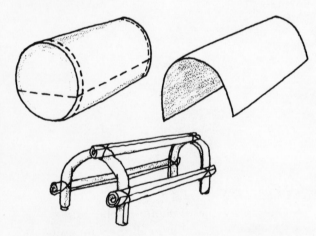

4. Roll most of the pulp between two pieces of wax paper to equal the size of the armature. Lift the pulp and drape it over the armature. It can be curved slightly to make an irregular contour. If any cracks appear, patch them with leftover pulp. For additional rough contours, apply bits of pulp with fingers. If there are to be such features as a waterfall or lake, be sure to make indentations or leave openings in the pulp.

5. Let outside dry; then turn over to let inside dry. If desired, cover the armature inside with more pulp or with pasted strips. But do be sure to cover all the sharp wire ends, even if nothing else is covered.

6. Make the waterfall and lake from crushed blue tissue paper. Attach it to the pulp with acrylic gloss medium. Brush more medium over it. Simulate water foam with streaks of white and lighter blue paint.

7. For the exposed rocky part of the mountain, leave the pulp its natural color. Paint the rest with acrylic gesso.

8. For snow areas, leave the gesso as is. For vegetation, paint various shades of green.

9. Rocks and boulders may be made from pulp, or from found stones, pebbles, or gravel. Attach to landscape with white glue.

10. Finish with acrylic matte varnish to retain the dull finish (except for the water which was previously coated with gloss medium).

PAPIER-MÂCHÉ TREES
(Color Plate 10)

A tree with many separate branches can be modeled on an armature of chicken wire. Cut the chicken wire with wire clippers at as many intersections as possible. With pliers shape the loose ends into branches. With the fingers cover all the exposed wires with bits of pulp. The wires are very sharp; only teens or adults who are experienced with these materials should make these trees.

Other trees can be modeled by hand, and children can do these. Narrow ones that taper at the top such as evergreens can be formed in one piece. Top-heavy ones cannot be made in one piece because the moist pulp trunk is too thin and weak to support the heavy top. Use either of the following methods:

• Mold the base and trunk first. When dry, mold and attach the top part to the trunk.

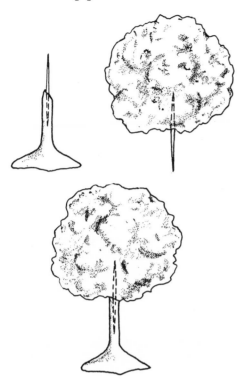

• Mold the base and trunk and put a toothpick halfway into the trunk. Mold the top and put another toothpick halfway into the top. Let both parts dry separately. When dry, remove both toothpicks, squirt a drop of glue into each hole, and reassemble with only one toothpick as a support.

Don't use up all the pulp in making trees. Always save a few pinches in a plastic bag in the refrigerator. They may be needed for patches if the tops and bottoms of trees don't meet exactly.

When dry, there are two options for finishing the foliage:

· Painting
· Pasting on crumpled bits of tissue paper

In either case, the trunks are painted; let a bit of the natural-colored pulp show through to simulate the shadings of real bark.

Painting is easier for children to do and is more durable. Set out several shades of green, and dab them on at random; trees should not be all one color. When dry, seal with a coat of acrylic matte varnish for a dull finish.

Crumpled bits of tissue or crepe paper add a lively look to the trees. They are not very durable, but it might be fun to do a couple. Select trees of simple shape, such as spheres or cones because the papers would obscure the shape of intricately branched trees. To do papered trees, crumple tiny bits of several shades of green paper. Brush some glue on the tree form, and press on a few bits of paper, either with the fingers or with tweezers. Do one small section at a time. When finished and dry, dab acrylic matte varnish over all.

Train stations and other buildings for the landscape may be made from milk cartons or other boxes. (See page 80 for information on using paper wrappings and printed details, and page 138 for information on using painted cartons and collaged details.)

ARMATURE COVERED WITH STRIPS

CHARACTER HANG-UPS
(*Color Plate 6*)

AGE: TEENS
TIME: HOURS WITH INTERVALS FOR
    DRYING

NECESSITIES:

- Two wire clothes hangers
- Newspaper strips
- 20 half-sheets of newspaper
- Tight-woven fabric, such as an old sheet
- Liquid starch
- Acrylic gesso
- Acrylic paints
- Acrylic varnish

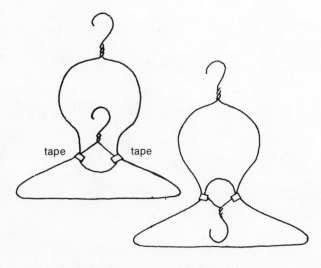

STEP-BY-STEP:

1. Make an armature by twisting two wire hangers together as illustrated.

2. Fill in the empty space by folding pasted strips around the wire edge.

3. The fastest way to build up a large flat surface is with pasted layers. Trace the outline of the hanger on a sheet of newspaper, and use that as a pattern to cut out 20 identical pieces. Make two stacks of 10 sheets each, with a layer of paste between each. Paste one stack onto the front of the covered armature, and the second stack onto the back. Let the whole thing dry, hanging in the sun, or lying in a warm oven with just the pilot light on.

4. For extra stiffness, apply a piece of fabric cut to the same pattern as the armature, and dipped in liquid starch, to the back and front. Use strips of the same fabric dipped in starch for binding the edges.

5. Cover the wet starch with a layer of dry paper strips. When that is dry, paste on at least three more layers of strips (or more if a thicker hanger is preferred).

6. When the entire thing is thoroughly dry, coat it with gesso and let it dry.

7. Paint a face on one side. The back can either be a duplicate face, a different face, or the back of the head. Another alternative is to paste on an enlarged photo of oneself or of a favorite star.

8. Finish with two coats of varnish, allowing plenty of drying time between coats.

JEWELRY

(Color Plates 4 and 5)

AGE: PRE-TEEN AND UP
TIME: MINUTES TO HOURS, PLUS INTER-
VAL FOR DRYING

Papier-mâché is so lightweight that it is ideal for making huge chunky jewelry, from meatball-sized beads to cable-thick bracelets. Techniques range from simple to complex.

PULP BEADS

(See Color Plate 5)

Roll pulp into balls and insert a toothpick all the way through to make a hole for later stringing. Beads that are painted with metallic gold paint look like gold nuggets.

STRIP BEADS

Cut pasted layers of paper into strips, shape into cubes, pyramids, or rings, and paint. String them together for beads, or use individually for earrings.

PULP BROOCHES

(See Color Plate 4 and 5)

Press pulp onto one side of a can lid and around the cut edge. If desired, an attractive button or fake jewel may be embedded. One of the photographed brooches was painted with metallic gold paint and dots of fluorescent paint, and sealed with clear plastic spray. The one with the embedded button has a design incised with a knife blade. Pin backings were pasted on back with contact cement.

PULP BRACELETS

Cut a ring of the desired width from a styrofoam cup. Depending on the circumference of the hand, cut the ring from the top of the cup or from lower down. Press pulp onto the outside of the band. Style a bracelet by painting with metallic silver paint and trim with yarn. The photographed bracelet was incised to match the pulp brooch; the set was painted and varnished with acrylics (see Color Plate 5.)

STRIP BRACELET

Use a jar or can as a mold for a bracelet.

Sprinkle with cornstarch so strips won't stick. Wrap with a newspaper strip of desired width. Add 6–8 layers of pasted strips or squares of newspaper. For extra strength, include at least one layer of kraft paper (supermarket bags) or construction paper. Seal with gesso. Decorate or paint. Varnish.

PULP COLLAR NECKLACE

A dress form can be used to mold an Egyptian-looking breastplate necklace. First cover the dress form with plastic wrap. Then roll out papier-mâché pulp to about $\frac{1}{2}''$ thickness and drape it on the dress form; it is especially important to get the neck curve right. Do not connect it at the center back.

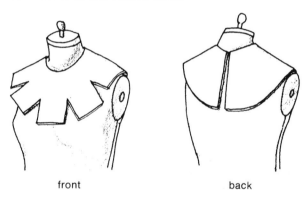

front   back

When dry, mark the shoulder seam line before lifting the entire piece from the dress form. Saw the pulp through the shoulder seam lines, and reattach the pieces with hinges with concealed pins. Paint the whole thing with metallic gold or silver paint. Decorate it by pasting on metallic cords and/or fake jewels.

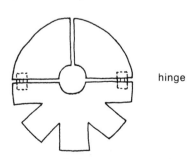

hinge

ON YOUR OWN

There is so much more that can be done with papier-mâché; in fact, nearly every item in this book could probably have been made from papier-mâché. Here are some more project ideas.

For children:

· A play tunnel or hideaway. Use an armature of chicken wire or mold it over a trash can protected with a plastic trash bag.
· Cover an old chair to become a "person" or "animal" chair. One or both "hands" can be turned palm up to hold a glass or snack plate.
· For papier-mâché puppets, see page 156.
· For papier-mâché maracas, see page 162.

Home furnishings:

· Make huge outdoor planters by covering the lower half of discarded trash cans.
· Make a headboard for a bed with pulp or strips over a plywood armature.

· Garage sales and flea markets are good sources for battered furniture to renew with papier-mâché techniques.

To go further into papier-mâché, these are two of the best specialized books:

Original Creations with Papier-Mâché, by Mildred Anderson.
New York: Sterling Publishing Co., 1972.
Excellent for furniture and room accessories. Assumes a knowledge of the basics.

Papier-Mâché Artistry, by Dona Z. Meilach.
New York: Crown Publishers, 1971.
Mostly decorative household accessories, but covers the widest variety of techniques in a well-organized way. From beginners to advanced.

Potatoes and Other Printables

Potato printing is often regarded as strictly a nursery-school activity, but it really is an all-age activity which can be as simple or as sophisticated as you want to make it. It can lead to printing with other materials and can reach its pinnacle in such graphic arts as lithography (stone printing), serigraphy (silk-screen printing), and collography (embossed printing).

But, begin at the beginning with potatoes!

Potatoes. Select a baking potato because it has less moisture than a general-purpose potato. Dry it out even more by letting the cut pieces stand an hour or two before printing with them. If eager to start immediately, at least stand the cut sides on a paper towel while assembling the papers and paints.

Papers. For beginning experiments use:
- Rough-surfaced papers like manila drawing paper or newsprint
- Newspaper pages with fine print, such as classified ads or stock market pages
- Supermarket bags
- Construction paper

For advanced work and projects use:
- Watercolor paper
- Rice paper (available in art supply stores)
- Tissue paper
- Fabrics

Paints. Use paints described below.

Tempera paints are best. A good way to set them up is in partitioned TV-dinner trays. In each section, put a paint pad of one of the following materials:
- A soft cloth, such as flannel, folded in eight layers (for the smoothest prints)
- A paper towel folded in eight layers
- A kitchen sponge (for the most textured prints)
- Two layers of felt (wool or wool-blend) wrapped around a wood block

Dampen the pad with water, pour on a bit of tempera, and brush it in. The idea is to have an ample quantity of pigment, but pigment should not be so thick on the surface that it produces messy blobs on prints. Paint pads make it necessary to apply a bit of pressure to make the pigment adhere to the potato and assure even prints. As the tempera dries out, occasionally brush a drop or two of water onto the surface of the pad.

Stamp pads are undoubtedly neater and easier to use than tempera. Their disadvantages are that the colors are more limited and more muted, and therefore not so interesting for young children to use. Older ones, who are doing small design work, however, may prefer the sharp, even impression it is possible to get with stamp pads.

Waterproof inks are very easy to use; simply pour a small amount into each section of a TV-dinner tray. But they should be restricted to careful children. They give a very smooth impression which some people like and others find monotonous.

Acrylic paints are best for most projects. They are thicker than tempera and require a different printing technique which eliminates the need for paint pads. Instead of dipping the potato stamper into the paint, brush the paint onto the printing surface of the potato. This will produce a thinner layer of paint and a better print.

Cutting Potato Stampers

There are two main techniques for making potato stampers. The essential element in both is that *the potato must not extend beyond the outline of the stamping shape.* It is essential to see the printing edges for accurate placement.

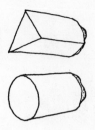

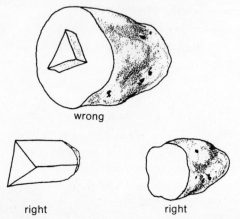

wrong

right   right

An ordinary kitchen paring knife is fine for most shapes, although a craft knife might be used for curves, or even canape cutters for fancy shapes. Naturally, a very young child should not do the cutting.

Method 1: Cut the potato in half lengthwise, and then into approximately 1″ crosswise slices. Make each piece into a different shape stamper, with the skin side serving as the handle. A discussion of shapes is included in the section on design development.

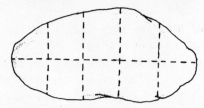

Method 2: Cut a thin slice off one end; use the larger piece as the stamper. When that surface is either used up, or becomes boring, or becomes discolored (as after an overnight stay), cut off another slice, and continue printing. The entire potato can be used by removing slices when necessary. This method is good for a preschooler's first trials because a little hand needs a large piece to hold; as finger coordination improves, children can gradually use smaller stampers. (For a young child, scrub the potato skin first.)

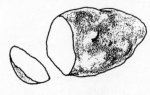

A variation of this slicing method can be used in a more sophisticated way. Gouge out a shallow shape from the potato surface; the resulting print will be a circle with a negative shape within. Cut off a slice, and gouge out a different shape. Continue as long as the potato lasts. This method is fine for experiments, or for someone who plans everything well in advance, because once a slice is removed, it's obviously impossible to go back to that shape again!

Sometimes an entire potato is used for only one stamper if a very large shape is required.

Potato   Print

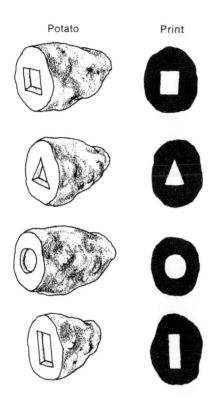

Designing potato prints

Potato printing is best suited to simple geometric shapes, which by repetition, combination, and overprinting can actually become quite elaborate. However, carving an intricate pattern into a potato is not the most effective use of the medium; styrofoam and aluminum foil plates better lend themselves to that technique (see pages 82–86).

Beginners, whether preschool or adult, can all start exactly the same way; how far each person goes in developing designs will depend on age, experience, and interest.

First, cut a thin slice from one end of the potato. Holding the larger piece, dip the cut end into paint, and print it. The need to dip every time or less frequently soon becomes obvious; the design can be controlled somewhat by heavier and lighter applications of paint. While getting the feel of the printing, first efforts might look like this: first row evenly spaced, then a offset-row design. Then, try overlapping. This is already a start to designing.

Techniques for printing with potatoes

There are two techniques; the selection depends on the age of the printer and on the effect desired.

• For preschoolers, and when a textured effect is preferred, press the potato into the pigment, then press it slowly and firmly onto the paper. Make a few trial prints on a scrap of paper to decide how much pigment and how much pressure are necessary, and whether it is necessary to dip *each* time, or whether several prints can be made from each paint dip. Preschoolers don't need a "scrap" paper and a "good" paper; for them, they are one and the same. In fact, anyone's "scrap" paper may be just as attractive as the "good" one; the spontaneous design is often more exciting than the planned one.

• For a smooth-textured print, and when the pigment is thick, brush the paint onto the potato, then press the potato onto the paper. New paint must be brushed on before making each print.

There are four elements through which variety can be provided:

- Shape of the potato stamper
- Placement of each impression
- Color of the pigment
- Color of the background

A three-year-old will be happy repeating the same shape and the same color for quite a while. He or she will provide as much variety as necessary by the placement of each impression. When the child seems to need something new, provide a new color paint. Preschoolers won't be scrupulous about keeping the colors separate, so a third color will eventually emerge. Either red or blue is a good first color because they are so bright; yellow is a good second color because when mixed with the first, it will yield an easily recognizable blend. (Red + yellow = orange; blue + yellow = green.)

An older person (or the three-year-old in a subsequent printing session) will be ready for a new shape. Cut the big potato piece as described in Method 1 under Cutting Potato Stampers (page 60), and make the first stamper with a 1″ square printing surface. For a youngster, cut the square larger, and don't distract him with any of the following techniques. He isn't yet interested in recognizable forms or designs; he just wants to experiment and see what happens.

Here is the way an older child, a teenager, or an adult might develop designs based on squares, first varying the placement of the squares. Later, adding new colors and creating new color combinations can be tried.

Next, cut the square diagonally to provide two right-angle triangles. This is probably the most versatile shape.

The next shape to try is a narrow rectangle.

These four shapes—the almost circular potato slice, the square, the triangle, and the rectangle—are the most versatile and the most useful ones for general design work. For pictorial work, some additional shapes may be useful:

- Circles (these are very difficult to cut free-hand; use a lemon juicer or canape cutter, if available)
- Crescents
- Ovals
- Narrow triangles

The next stage in design development might be to cut away a simple shape from within a larger shape and to work simple variations on that, sometimes based on color, sometimes based on placement.

Then see how just a few simple shapes can be repeated or combined into more complex patterns and pictures.

By the time a preschooler is finished printing, he or she is likely to have as much paint on the hands as on the printing paper. Before cleaning up, let the child make a handprint on a paper plate. When dry, write his or her name and the date on back, and varnish it. It's a nice keepsake, and children like this "handy" proof of how much they have grown. It's much easier for them to compare their own hand with a handprint than to compare their own height with a mark on a wall.

If there are some leftover paints from experiments that will have to be discarded anyway, play around by printing one color after another without wiping the stamper each time. The variegated results will be delightful; in fact, these spontaneous prints may be more appealing than some of the meticulously planned ones.

Print Makers Other Than Potatoes ✳ ✳ ✳ ✳ ✳ ✳ ✳ ✳ ✳ ✳ ✳ ✳

Printing with fruit, vegetables, and kitchen utensils

Any firm fruit or vegetable can be used as a print stamper. Older children are often quite imaginative in incorporating these "found" shapes into both representational pictures and caricatures.

- An orange cut crosswise (Be sure to blot the excess juice before inking.)
- A pear or apple cut either crosswise or lengthwise (The pit pattern is interesting both ways.)
- Carrot or parsnip (Cut about an inch below the top and leave the stems attached for a handle.)

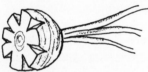

- Cross-cuts of celery make lovely crescents.

- Broccoli and cauliflower (Cut one stalk or floret lengthwise down the center. By brushing brown paint on bottom and other colors on top, trees or flowering shrubs can be printed.)

- Carrot tops, parsley, and dill prints look like foliage.
- Mushrooms and artichokes (when not exorbitantly expensive) make interesting prints when cut down the center. (If printing with food coloring, cut away the colored part of the artichoke, and the rest will be agreeable to look at and safe to eat.)

- Green beans cut lengthwise (An overmature bean with fully developed seeds makes the most interesting print.)

Kitchen utensils and supplies often provide needed shapes:

- Potato masher
- Bottle caps and jar covers
- Corks
- Forks
- Whole cloves (the heads are good for making dots)
- Sponges (One sponge can be cut into enough pieces to provide a variety of shapes.)
- Cans, jars, and cardboard tubes (Wrap with corrugated cardboard or a string design.)

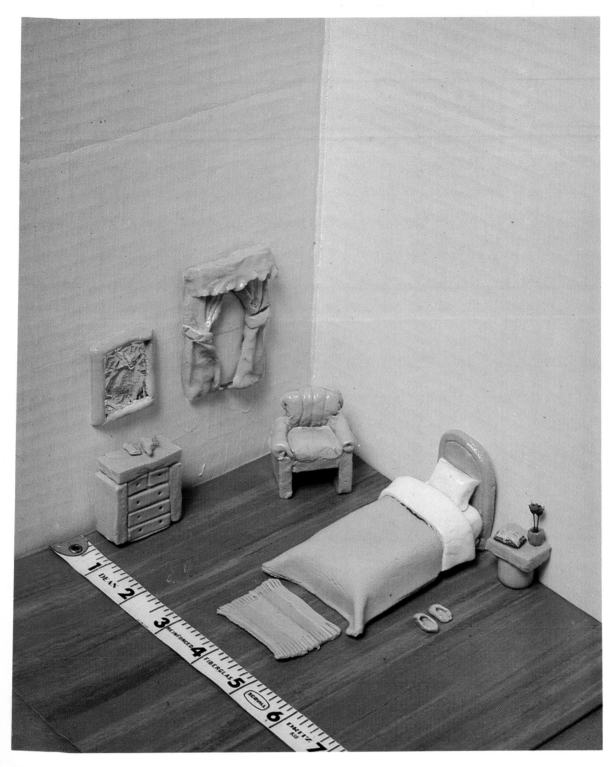

COLOR PLATE 1
Miniature Furniture, page 33.

COLOR PLATE 2
Lasagne Loonies, page 93.

COLOR PLATE 3

1. Picture Frame, page 26. **2.** Flower Plaque Mosaics, page 37. **3.** Plastic Can Lid Hanging (Coaster), page 144. **4.** Seed Mosaic Plaque, page 23. **5.** Rope Mirror Frame, page 94. **6.** Little Girl Plaque, page 21. **7.** Sampler Plaque, page 103. **8.** Artichoke Plaque, page 22. **9.** Mushroom and Peapod Plaque, page 22. **10.** Eggshell Mosaic Plate, page 123.

COLOR PLATE 4

1. Cantalope Seed Pin, page 107. **2.** Four-Pointed Pendant, page 31. **3.** Star-Shaped Pendant, page 30. **4.** Papier-Mâché Brooch, page 57. **5.** Embossed Pendant, page 20. **6.** Yarn Decorated Pendant, page 20. **7.** Modern Aluminum Foil Brooch, page 147. **8.** Seed Inlaid Pendants, page 20. **9.** Metallic Pendant, page 31. **10.** Melon Seed Pendant, page 107. **11.** Orange-Bordered Pendant, page 31.

COLOR PLATE 5

1. Marbleized Pasta Beads, page 89. **2.** Cornstarch Disk Beads, page 31. **3.** Cornstarch Teardrop Twists, page 32. **4.** Cornstarch Twisted Dangles, page 32. **5.** Rotelle Pendant Necklace, page 95. **6.** and **7.** Papier-Mâché Pin and Bracelet, page 57. **8.** Pop-Top Belt Buckle, page 20. **9.** and **10.** Aluminum Foil Pendant and Bracelet, page 147. **11.** Cornstarch Clay Collar Necklace, page 32. **12.** Wishbone Necklace, page 131. **13.** Ditalini Necklace, page 96. **14.** Papier-Mâché Beads, page 57. **15.** Marbleized Pasta Beads, page 89.

COLOR PLATE 6

1. Character Hang-Ups, page 56. **2.** Foil Wrapped Bottle, page 146. **3.** Seed Covered Bookend, page 106. **4.** Crayon Resist Container, page 141. **5.** Striped Container, page 46. **6.** Pencil Holder, page 45. **7.** Seed Covered Flowerpots, page 106. **8.** Seed Paperweight, page 104.

COLOR PLATE 7
1. Redecorated Table, page 47. **2.** Pasta Pillow, page 97. **3.** Painted Snack Bowl, page 48. **4.** Pasta Shell Tree, page 92. **5.** Plastic Can Lid Coasters, page 144. **6.** Bread Basket, page 25. **7.** Paper Cut-Out Snack Bowl, page 52. **8.** Mock Tortoiseshell Tray, page 144. **9.** Cardboard Tube Napkin Rings, page 142. **10.** Pasta Sampler, page 92.

COLOR PLATE 8

1. Medallioned Black Egg, page 116. **2.** Embossed Metallic Egg, page 115. **3.** Metallic Eggs, page 115. **4.** Découpage Egg, page 118. **5.** Caged Eggs, page 120. **6.** Mosaic Eggs, page 119. **7.** Dotty Eggs, page 117. **8.** Food Coloring Marbleized Egg, page 121. **9.** Tissue Collage Egg, page 118. **10.** Beribboned Glitter Egg, page 115. **11.** Sequined Egg, page 116. **12.** Child's Tempera-Painted Egg. **13.** Marbleized Eggs, page 121. **14.** Pseudo-Pysanky Egg, page 123.

COLOR PLATE 9
Egg Carton Ornaments, page 142.

COLOR PLATE 10

1. Little Toys—Airplanes, page 19. **2.** Model Train Landscape, page 53. **3.** Milk Carton Wrap-Arounds, page 139. **4.** Papier-Mâché Trees, page 54. **5.** Little Toys—Cars, page 19. Play Buildings, page 80 and 138.

COLOR PLATE 11

1. Paper Plate Puppets, page 153. **2.** Papier-Mâche Puppet, page 156. **3.** Wooden Spoon Puppet, page 150. **4.** Cardboard Tube Puppet, page 154. **5.** Fireman's Hat, page 49. **6.** Large Can Drum, page 158 and Yarn Wrapped Drum, page 159. **7.** Drumsticks, page 160. **8.** Tamborine, page 162. **9.** Balloon Maraca, page 162. **10.** Light Bulb Maracas, page 163. **11.** Finger Puppets, page 152.

COLOR PLATE 12

1. Fluorescent Crayon Hot-Tray Painting, page 134. **2.** Food Color Marbleized Paper, page 126. **3.** Crayon Hot Tray Painting, page 134. **4.** Aluminum Foil Printmaking, page 85. **5.** Potato Printed Gift Paper, page 77. **6.** Dip-Dyed Papers, page 126. **7.** Potato Printed Gift Paper, page 77. **8.** Gift Box, page 78. **9.** Book Cover, page 79. **10.** Vegetable Printed Notepaper, page 64. **11.** Herb Notepaper, page 131. **12.** Food Color Finger Paintings, page 125.

Printing with rollers

Use rollers to paint repeat patterns.

NECESSITIES:
- Old or toy rolling pin (or next three items)
- Cardboard tube
- Empty thread spool to fit inside tube
- Dowel to fit inside thread spool (Tinkertoy rod is exactly right)
- Wrappings to provide texture, e.g., yarn, corrugated paper
- White glue
- Tempera paint and brush
- Metal tray and printing brayer (optional)

STEP-BY-STEP:

1. Assemble cardboard tube roller as illustrated. Use it like a rolling pin.

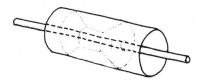

2. Glue printing elements on. String may be arranged into a curved pattern. Corrugated paper may be wrapped around the entire roller, or just portions of it.

3. Use one of these methods to put paint on roller:
- Brush it on with a paint brush.
- Roll the paint on a tray with a brayer to distribute a uniformly thin layer. Roll the

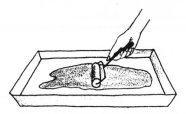

roller back and forth in the paint until it is evenly covered.

4. Roll the roller on the paper to print it.

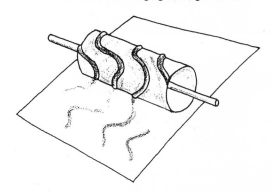

PROJECTS

GIFT WRAPPING PAPERS
(*Color Plate 12*)

AGE: ALL AGES
TIME: MINUTES

This is an activity the entire family can enjoy together. Even the completely random hodge-podge that a preschooler is likely to print will be attractive enough to use for wrapping gifts. It's never too early for a child to learn that a gift is more meaningful when the giver puts something of himself or herself into it, rather than just buying everything ready-made. And it's never too soon to acknowledge a child's efforts by including them in family gift-giving.

NECESSITIES:
- Potato stampers
- Paints and/or stamp pads
- Papers (newspapers with small type, such as stock market pages, for preschoolers; construction paper, white or colored tissue paper, non-shiny shelving for older children and adults)

STEP-BY-STEP:

1. Print papers according to the instructions under printing techniques, page 61.

2. When using tissue paper, keep the paint quite dry; otherwise, the paper may wrinkle and the color will probably bleed.

3. Keep the potato stamper shapes simple; the multiple repetitions will form the design and pattern.

4. The negative spaces are as important as the printed areas, as can be seen in the paper printed entirely with triangles.

ON YOUR OWN
• Print enough gift wrap paper to have a supply on hand at all times.
• Print gift wrap paper with fruit, vegetables, kitchen utensils, or rollers.

GIFT BOX

(*Color Plate 12*)

AGE: PRE-TEENS AND UP
TIME: MINUTES

A plain white gift box from the 5&10 can be covered with colored tissue paper, then potato-printed afterward in a pattern designed to fit the box.

This is a simplified method of covering a box, which uses folded corners rather than cut corners. It is much easier for children to master because there is no chance of a wrong cut which would ruin the paper. It's a good idea to practice by covering the bottom of the box before doing the lid.

NECESSITIES:
- Plain white box
- Colored tissue paper
- Potato stamper
- Tempera paint
- Shellac

STEP-BY-STEP:

1. Turn the box bottom upside down on a table. Place the tissue paper over it, and use the edges as a guide to folding the indicated lines. The paper will be folded in a tic-tac-toe pattern.

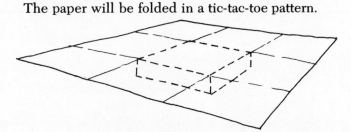

2. Cut at a distance from the inner rectangle equal to the depth of the box plus $\frac{1}{2}''$.

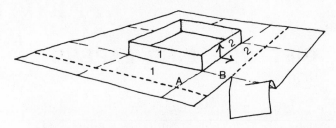

3. Now lay the box upright on the paper. Fold side 1 of the paper up against side 1 of the box so that line A meets corner A.

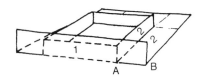

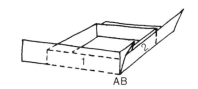

4. Bend the corner piece inward against box side 2 until paper side 2 folds up against the box and line B meets line A.

5. Fold the ½" surplus over the edge of the box to the inside, and secure the corner with clear tape.

6. Repeat with the other three corners.

7. Cover the box lid the same way.

8. Print the box with a small border print.

9. To strengthen the paper and give it a more finished look, seal it with a coat of shellac (this should be done by an adult). (If acrylic paint is used, seal the paper with acrylic medium.)

BOOK COVER

(Color Plate 12)

AGE: TEENS AND ADULTS
TIME: MINUTES, PLUS MANY INTERVALS
FOR DRYING.

An ordinary address book from the 5&10 can be enriched with a tissue paper cover to make it a lovely gift item. Because the tissue paper is transparent, the same color book and tissue paper should be used.

NECESSITIES:
- Address book
- Colored tissue paper
- Sponge for printing
- Acrylic paint
- Acrylic gloss medium
- Paper clip or spring clothespin to hang book for drying

STEP-BY-STEP:

1. Cut out tissue paper ¾" larger all around than the open book.

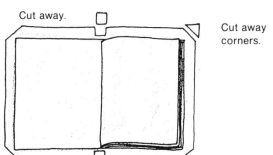

2. Fold the tissue over the book if the exact placement of the design is important. The illustrated book is left unprinted over the area where the words "Addresses Telephones" from the original book are to show through.

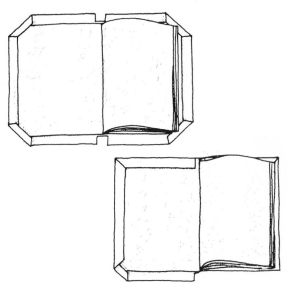

3. Remove tissue from book, and print the paper; this print was made in acrylic paint with a sponge rectangle.

4. When the paint is dry, place the book on the paper and cut as indicated.

5. Coat the book with acrylic gloss medium and cover it with the tissue.

6. On the inside cover, brush the edges with acrylic medium, and fold the paper overhang to the inside. First fold the corner diagonally, then the straight edges to make mitered corners.

7. Now coat the entire cover with medium, and hang it to dry by clipping the inner pages and attaching the clip to a rod or hanger.

8. For a more elegant look, make endpapers of matching or blending tissue. Cut one sheet of tissue just ⅛″ smaller than the combined size of the inside cover and first page. Apply the same way as the cover, with medium both under and over the tissue. Hang to dry as before.

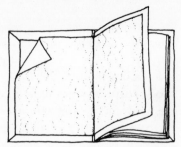

ON YOUR OWN

• These methods of covering books and boxes can be used on any size items and with any kind of decorative papers, as well as fabrics.

• Other items can be covered as well. To cover a notepad, paste a pad of paper onto a piece of cardboard large enough to fold over to form a front cover. Cover it with tissue and proceed as for the address book.

PLAY TOWN
(Color Plate 10)

Playing out scenes of city or suburban life has always appealed to children. They re-enact life as they see it or as they wish it would be, and it is a very important part of social development between the ages of three and ten. There are many commercial toys of this type, but the play is so much more satisfying and meaningful when a child can decide just which stores and buildings should be included and how they should look.

AGE: PRESCHOOL (WITH HELP) TO PRE-TEENS
TIME: MINUTES TO HOURS

NECESSITIES:
· Milk and cream cartons, rinsed and dried
· Strong paper (e.g. supermarket bags)
· White glue
· Potato stampers
· Paint
· Varnish or acrylic medium (optional)

STEP-BY-STEP:
1. Cut and shape cartons as needed.

- Cartons with peaked tops are good for church steeples, official public buildings, and barns.
- To change peaked-top cartons into flat-top cartons, cut, fold, and tape them as illustrated.

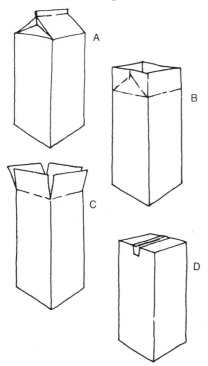

- To make a ranch house roof, cut a carton the same size as the house diagonally lengthwise.

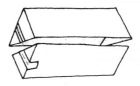

2. Brush glue on cartons, and wrap them in paper.

3. Use potato stamps for windows, doors, roof tiles, bricks, shrubbery, and other building details.

4. If the buildings are ones that a child uses frequently in play, they should be sealed. Tempera paints should be sealed (by an adult) with varnish. Acrylic paints can be coated with acrylic medium.

NOTE: For other ways of making buildings, see Milk Carton Village on pages 138–139.

STATIONERY AND NOTEPAPER
(Color Plate 12)

AGE: PRE-TEENS AND UP
TIME: MINUTES

NECESSITIES:
- Blank notepaper or stationery
- Potato stampers
- Other stampers suggested on page 64
- Paint and brush

STEP-BY-STEP:

1. For abstract designs, cut potato stampers into desired shapes.

2. For nature prints, try a carrot-top or a cauliflower floret for a tree.

3. Make small corner prints or border prints on the notepaper or stationery. An imprint on the flap of the envelope is a nice touch.

ON YOUR OWN
- Imprint bookmarks cut from oaktag poster board. The size can range from $1\frac{1}{2}''$–$2''$ wide and from $6''$–$8''$ long.
- For more delicate designs, print with stamp pads instead of paint.

Fish prints. There are other things to print that require different techniques . . . for instance,

Potatoes and Other Printables 81

the traditional Japanese fish prints. Imagine what would happen if a fish were pressed into paint and pushed down on a piece of paper! In this case, brush the fish with paint and lay the paper on it, rubbing gently with the hand. Before removing the paper, lift one end (while holding the other down firmly) and peek under it to see if a dark enough impression has transferred to the paper. If not, replace the paper and rub again before removing it. Fish prints are often beautiful enough to mat and frame, either individually or in groups.

Rubbing. There's also the possibility of wanting to print something which would be spoiled by putting paint on it. In this case, a technique known as rubbing can be used. In its simplest form, it consists of putting a paper on a textured object and rubbing a crayon lightly over the paper so that only the high parts are recorded in color. Try this on a grater, on cane chair seats, on baskets, air-conditioner vents, and other things around the house.

—A landscape or still life drawing can be made by filling in each area with an appropriately textured rubbing.

—A fine game to develop children's perceptions is to prepare a series of texture rubbings without the child, and then see if he or she can figure out the object on which they were made. A child can also provide adults with some puzzlers of the same type!

The technique of rubbing can be carried to a fine art. Gravestone rubbings and manhole cover rubbings are the best-known forms of an increasingly popular hobby.

Styrofoam Printmaking * *

One form of printmaking based on repetition of small shapes was explored with potatoes. Styrofoam is used for an entirely different kind of printing based on pictorial representation, all-over pattern, and more complex shapes. The prints are beautiful framed and make distinctive note cards, gift toys, stationery, holiday greeting cards, and invitations.

There are two steps to styrofoam printing:

1. Making a plate by making indentations in those areas of the styrofoam which are not to be printed.

2. Making a print by coating the surface of the styrofoam with paint or ink and pressing the paper against it.

MAKING THE PLATES

First experiments with styrofoam plates will be random scratching with a stylus or ballpoint pen with point retracted, or pressing interestingly shaped objects into the styrofoam.

NECESSITIES:
- Four or more styrofoam trays, with raised rims cut away
- One or more of the following for texturing the styrofoam:
    Claw end of a hammer
    Tip of a meat baster
    Bottle caps
    Blade of a knife used for making crinkle-cut vegetable slices (for use by older children, teens, and adults)
    Screw heads
- Tools to draw, scratch, or stab with, such as:
    Paper clip
    Scissors blades, closed and opened (for use by older children, teens, and adults)
    Screwdriver tip
    Fingernails
    Pencil point
    Needle (for use by older children, teens, and adults)
    Toothpick
    Fork
    Comb
- Tool for gouging, such as linoleum cutter or craft knife (for use only by teens and adults)

STEP-BY-STEP:
(Each step requires a separate styrofoam tray.)

1. Use one of the drawing objects to divide the styrofoam tray into nine sections (like a tic-tac-toe grid). Fill each section with a different kind of texture by scratching or stabbing with one of the suggested objects.

2. Use a ballpoint pen with point retracted to make a line drawing.

3. Make a second line drawing (it could be the same as the previous one or different), but this time add appropriate textures to some of the blank areas, using one or more of the techniques discovered in step 1.

4. Cut a styrofoam tray into pieces; rearrange the shapes and glue them to a plywood backing leaving empty spaces between.

MAKING THE PRINTS

PRINTING METHOD ONE
AGE: PRESCHOOL (WITH ADULT HELP)
TIME: MINUTES

The easiest method, recommended for younger children, uses tempera.

NECESSITIES:
- Tempera paint and brush
- Printing paper (rough papers like newsprint and construction paper)
- Textured styrofoam printing plate

STEP-BY-STEP:

1. Brush the paint on the styrofoam printing plate. Use enough to completely cover the styrofoam, but not so much that it fills the depressions.

2. Lay the printing paper on top of the plate and press firmly and evenly in a circular motion with the fingertips or with the heel of the hand. (The reason the styrofoam is not turned upside down onto the paper is that the thickness and softness of the styrofoam would prevent as

strong an impression as when pressing on the paper directly.)

3. Before removing the paper, hold one half firmly and lift the other half to check whether the impression is dark enough. If it is, remove the paper and let it dry. Otherwise, replace the paper and rub harder.

PRINTING METHOD TWO
AGE: PRE-TEENS AND UP
TIME: MINUTES

NECESSITIES:
· Water-soluble block printing ink
· Soft rubber brayer
· Metal tray (such as cookie sheet or jelly-roll pan), or a sheet of glass
· Printing paper
· Large wooden or metal spoon (optional)

STEP-BY-STEP:
1. Squeeze about an inch of printing ink onto the tray, and roll the brayer back and forth and sideways until a thin layer of ink is evenly distributed on both the brayer and the tray.

2. Roll the brayer on the styrofoam until it is evenly inked. If necessary, roll the brayer on the tray again to pick up more ink.

3. Follow steps 2 and 3 under the instructions for printing method one. For a deeper, smoother print, rub the printing paper with the back of a spoon.

ON YOUR OWN
• For printing with two or more colors with tempera, brush each desired color on the appropriate part of the printing plate, and then print as usual.
• Some styrofoam trays have an embossed grid pattern which can be used as a ready-made separate plate for a background.
• All techniques for styrofoam printing apply equally well to linoleum block printing, which would be an appropriate next material for more advanced printmaking.
• Prints may be used for holiday greeting cards and for invitations.

ALUMINUM FOIL PRINTMAKING
(*Color Plate 12*)

The difference between styrofoam printmaking in the previous section and aluminum foil printmaking to be done now is this: a styrofoam printing plate is made by incising the texture into the plate, while an aluminum foil printing plate is made by glueing (collaging) the textures onto the base.

NECESSITIES:
- Cardboard base
- Textured objects, such as:
    - Crushed eggshells
    - Window screening
    - Plastic berry baskets
    - Corduroy, lace, mesh, burlap
    - Small cardboard shapes
    - Thread or cord
- White glue
- Aluminum foil
- Water-base block printing ink (preferable) or acrylic or tempera paint
- Printing paper (absorbent, non-shiny)
- Newspapers, paper towels, plain newsprint or other scrap paper

STEP-BY-STEP:
1. *Prepare the printing plate.*

    a. Cut the cardboard base to the desired size and glue on it either a random assortment of textural materials, or materials whose textures look like what they are supposed to represent.

    b. When the glue is dry, wrap the plate with a piece of aluminum foil, dull side out, that is large enough to fold over to cover the back. The foil may either be pulled tight and smooth or may be wrinkled slightly for additional texture.

2. *Prepare the printing area.* Put 20 or more thicknesses of newspaper on the floor and cover with plain newsprint or other clean scrap paper.

3. *Prepare the printing paper.* Hold it under running water until saturated, then remove excess moisture with paper towels. Keep paper covered with damp paper towels until ready to use.

4. *Prepare printing plate* by one of these methods:

    a. *Embossed printing* (printing without ink) will simply reveal the texture and requires no inking.

    b. *Relief printing* (printing only the raised surface) requires the plate to be inked as described in the second method of styrofoam printing (page 84).

    c. *Collography* (printing the entire textured surface) requires the plate to be inked with the fingertips to insure that ink is rubbed into all the crevices. Variations in the texture of the final print are obtained by rubbing off more or less of the ink from the highest parts of the surface.

5. *Make the print.* On top of the newsprint-covered printing area, put the following, in order:

    The printing plate, face up
    The printing paper
    Another piece of clean newsprint

    If the plate is smaller than the sole of your shoe, step on it and roll the shoe sole on it with a firm heavy motion. If the plate is too large, put a heavy book or piece of wood between the printing paper and clean newsprint, and step on all parts of it for a few minutes.

6. Remove the print and set it on clean paper to dry. Repeat steps 3, 4, and 5 for as many prints as desired.

ON YOUR OWN
- If an etching press is available, it will of course provide more pressure on the plate and will therefore make a more professional-looking print than can be made by standing on it.
- Teens and adults who have had some printing experience may want to try the oil-based printing inks.
- A multi-color print can be made by rubbing different color inks on different areas of the plate.

Pasta Potpourri

Walk down the pasta aisle of the supermarket and take a package of every shape that catches your fancy. You and your family will find fascinating, and perhaps surprising, uses for all of them. Some of the ones referred to in this chapter are illustrated below.

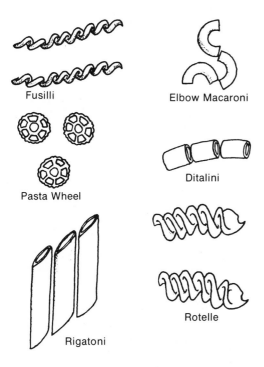

Fusilli

Elbow Macaroni

Pasta Wheel

Ditalini

Rigatoni

Rotelle

A three- to five- year-old who had already had experience in collage (pasting papers onto a background) will be ready to enjoy the challenge of pasting three-dimensional shapes. Provide a paper plate or styrofoam tray, an assortment of medium to large size pasta shapes, and a pot of paste. The child will work completely spontaneously, with no attempt at orderly arrangement. For variety, provide a sheet of bright or dark-colored construction paper as background.

A slightly older child will be more selective about which shapes to select and where to place them. The child may build a construction upward from the paper. It will be necessary to use white glue instead of paste.

A still older child will find these pasta pieces reminiscent of other things with other uses, and will begin to see whether a preconceived idea can be worked out in pasta. Bow ties may suggest butterflies; shells may become snails; twists may be transformed into caterpillars. At this stage, a child may want to paint the finished pasta creations.

Beginning in the pre-teen years, children may be ready for more structured pasta projects. They need to be reminded that the longer and thinner the pasta shapes, the more brittle they are. Pasta is more suited to decorative than functional articles that will get hard use.

Pasting has been mentioned. Other techniques are painting, stringing, stitchery, and modeling. Modeling? Yes, indeed!

Modeling. The craft use of pasta does not have to be restricted to its raw state. Pasta can be cooked and molded while soft to a preferred shape, and then allowed to harden again. This technique works especially well with pasta which comes in long strands (spaghetti, linguine, lasagne, and spiraled fusilli).

Cook a few strands at a time (three or four lasagne, 10–12 of the others) according to the package directions. Don't undercook, or it will still be brittle; don't overcook, or it will be too soft to manipulate easily. When done, add enough cold water to the pot to bring the contents to comfortable handling temperature.

Take one piece out of the pot and put it on a

paper towel for a few moments to absorb excess water before working with it. Keep the rest in the water to remain soft. Work on lightly-oiled aluminum foil, and when each piece is shaped, put it on another sheet of oiled foil to prevent the pasta from sticking as it dries. These are some of the uses for modeling cooked pasta.

Spaghetti and *linguine* can be used to write names, make curlicues, and do any kind of line drawing. Some children enjoy making caricature faces; others prefer animals or more complicated items like musical notation. The strands can be threaded with raw ditalini before shaping them.

Two *fusilli* strands can be twined together into a "two-ply rope" strong enough to be looped into a circle, knotted into a bow, or curved in other ways. The twisting can be interrupted at intervals to give a link effect. Raw ditalini has too small a hole to thread on fusilli, but cooked ditalini will fit.

Lasagne can be cut with scissors or a craft knife into silhouette shapes, which are suitable for wall plaques. With ripple-edged lasagne, the edge can be cut off separately and twisted into circles or bows, or incorporated into the design.

Depending on thickness, cooked pasta takes anywhere from overnight to two days to harden completely. The best way to dry flat pieces so they remain flat, and yet let the air reach them, is to dry them between two flat sheets of screen. An adequate substitute is two cake-drying racks with the wires at right angles to each other. The screens or racks should be lightly oiled first.

A three-dimensional piece will have to be dried on a foil-covered tray. Turn the pieces over occasionally to let air reach both sides equally. It will turn moldy if not exposed to air during drying.

Painting. The painting method chosen will depend on which is preferred: rich color or easy application. Unfortunately, both can't be achieved with any one product.

If ease of application is more important, completely assemble the project first, then dip it into:

FOOD COLORING SOLUTION
- $\frac{1}{2}$ CUP BOILING WATER
- 1 TEASPOON VINEGAR (SO THE DYE WON'T RUB OFF)
- 20 OR MORE DROPS OF FOOD COLORING

Let the liquid cool, at room temperature or in the refrigerator, before dipping the strung-up pasta pieces into it. (Hot water would soften the pieces and make them gummy.) The longer the pasta is submerged, the darker the color will become. Hang to dry.

The color of the pasta itself will always show through a transparent dye such as food coloring, weakening the color and imparting a straw-colored undertone to everything. The one exception is cooked lasagna, which takes on rich, deep, gem-like tones after 20–30 minutes. For some reason other shapes of cooked pasta don't do as well.

If beautiful color is the primary interest, use *fluorescent tempera paints*, also known as "day-glo" and "hot colors." They are not water-proof and would require sealing, a separate step which is rather inconvenient with pasta. The solution is to let the paints stand until the thick part has settled on the bottom. Pour off the watery liquid on top and replace it with acrylic medium (glossy or matte, depending on whether shiny or dull finish is preferred). The paint will then be as permanent as any acrylic paint.

Alternative paints, which are more satisfactory for larger shapes than small ones, are:

Tempera paints, which go on beautifully, but must be sealed with a coat of shellac.

Acrylic paints, whose only disadvantage is that the colors are not as rich as the fluorescents.

Airplane enamels, which have a good gloss but whose colors look muted. The metallics, however, are excellent.

These alternatives are especially good for easy-to-handle, larger shapes like macaroni tubes. A particularly effective technique is to paint the tubes a solid background color and allow to dry. Then take two or three additional colors and either dot them on with a toothpick, or swirl them in with a knife blade until they marbleize. Depending on the colors and type of paints used, the beads can be made to resemble Venetian glass, enameled metal, or Byzantine mosaics.

The nicest paint ideas come from trial experiments. If planning to make a string of beads some day with large macaroni tubes, keep a supply of them on hand so that whenever bits of paint are left over from other projects, they can be used in bead experiments. Try rolling the tubes on a palette that has several paints on it. (Color Plate 5).

Elaborately-painted beads like these need only to be strung simply on a corresponding shade of rug yarn.

If painting individual pieces of pasta before assembling a project, try to find plastic straws or pipe cleaners onto which the shapes will fit snugly; this way a whole group can be painted at a time. For instance, cocktail straws are just right for the ditalini shape; regular drinking straws fit through the macaroni tubes. Here is one set-up for painting using plasticene clay as a holder.

If nothing fits exactly, try stringing shapes on cord or thread, stretched like a clothesline. As a last resort, hold individual pieces in the hand and paint one part at a time.

Whatever method used, be sure to paint more pieces than seem necessary to allow for the inevitable breakages, or a revised plan requiring additional pieces.

Cooked and modeled pasta pieces are painted after they are assembled.

Stringing. Pasta is ideal for an introduction to beadcraft. Any shape that has a hole in it can, of course, be strung on a cord or piece of yarn. But that's only the beginning; even shapes *without* holes can be strung!

Threading beads is one of the essential co-ordination skills that young children must develop, and most children are ready for it between the age of two and three. Macaroni tubes about $1\frac{1}{2}''$ long and about $\frac{3}{8}''$ diameter are a fine size if the child *has passed the stage of putting everything in his mouth.* (Otherwise, he might bite the pasta and possibly choke on it.)

Give a little child a pile of macaroni tubes and a long shoelace with covered ends. It looks like play, but the child is really learning. First, there's the coordination practice. In addition, in stringing one bead at a time, he or she is doing some rudimentary counting, not with the names of numerals, of course, but with the concept of "one more," and "one more," and "one more."

Older children and adults can start practicing beadcraft with ditali or ditalini (short cylinders) and a cord about half the diameter of the hole. If something soft is used, like a 4-ply knitting worsted, thread it through a tapestry needle, or wrap tape around the ends to make a hard tip. Or use shoelaces.

Horizontal stringing is the ordinary kind.

Add interest to it by using a contrasting color yarn and making knots between the beads.

Vertical stringing is done with a double cord, looped through each bead from opposite directions. (The cord is loose in the illustrations for clarity. In actual practice, cords should be pulled snugly.)

It looks like: Stringing Pattern:

It can be combined with horizontal beading in several ways.

It looks like: Stringing Pattern:

Colors can be combined for a checkerboard effect.

It looks like: Stringing Pattern

Three or even more rows can be strung together.

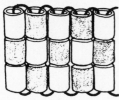

Spiral shapes can be wrapped with cord which, when pulled tight, will hold the spiral securely.

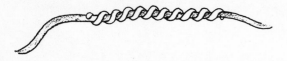

There is at least one shape, rotelle, which is a double spiral so that a cord wrapped around it goes in every other groove; at the bottom it can be turned around to come up through the skipped grooves. Tie the piece at the top to produce a pendant that can be threaded onto a necklace between other beads.

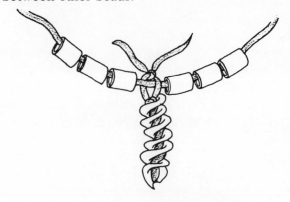

Stitchery. Pasta can be used like beads to add texture to stitchery. Only the smaller pieces are used because they are less likely to break. Ditalini, small wheels, and elbow macaroni offer a good variety of shapes. If they are to be colored, they must be painted before stitching.

It is best to stitch with tapestry wool or knitting worsted because their thickness is appropriate to the pasta holes. The easiest fabrics to use are loosely-woven ones like hopsacking, monk's cloth, and burlap; with these, a large-eyed, blunt-tipped tapestry needle can be used. Felt comes in such an array of beautiful colors that many people like to stitch on that, even though it is a bit more difficult and requires a sharp-tipped crewel needle.

Threading a needle can present some difficulties depending on the thickness of the yarn and the size of the needle. When using thread for stitchery, simply push the thread through the eye of the needle.

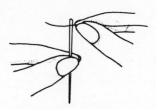

For thicker threads and yarns, crease yarn by folding the yarn and pulling against the needle. Then, push the crease through the eye of the needle.

When yarns are difficult to thread, fold a tiny rectangle of paper in half. Place the yarn end in the paper and squeeze shut. Push the paper and yarn through the eye of the needle.

Work will be neater if the fabric is put in an embroidery hoop.

These are some of the stitches into which pasta can be incorporated:

· Running stitch

· Satin stitch

· Couching stitch

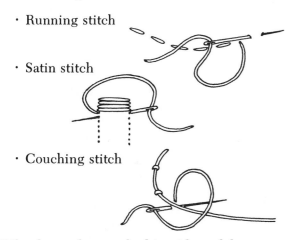

Wheels can be attached in either of these ways:

· With a french knot

· With an overstitch around the edges.

Elbow macaroni is slightly more difficult because a needle cannot be curved through it, nor is yarn stiff enough to be pushed through it. It is necessary to use a very stiff button and carpet thread, and to keep threading and unthreading the needle before and after each stitch.

1. Thread the needle and bring it up from the back of the fabric to the front.

2. Remove the needle and push the thread through the macaroni.

3. Rethread the needle and stitch down through the fabric to the back, and then from back to front. Repeat steps 2 and 3 until all the macaroni is in place.

4. To prevent the macaroni pieces from lifting up like arches in the middle, make a stitch across the center of each with either matching or contrasting yarn.

Several other stitches are useful to know because they combine well with pasta stitchery, even though they are not especially good for attaching purposes.

· Chain stitch

· Cross stitch

Experiment with different combinations of pasta and stitches with different colors of yarn and fabric. If all the experiments are done on the

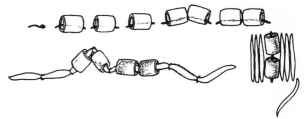

same size or shape pieces, they can eventually be combined into a pillow or a wall hanging. Or they can be appliquéd onto a solid-color bedspread or quilt.

(To appliqué, sew the piece onto a background, using either a blanket stitch (if the stitching is to show). Or, a slipstitch (if it is *not* to show).

The photographed sampler (Color Plate 7) was done as follows (beginning from the center):

1. Pasta wheel attached with French knot
2. Ring of satin stitches
3. Ring of elbow macaroni, fastened at centers with stitch superimposed on satin stitches with same yarn
4. Ring of ditalini
5. Ring of chain stitches
6. The felt circle on which the stitching was done was merely pasted with white glue on a larger felt circle to conceal the stitches onto back.

PROJECTS

PASTA SHELL TREE
(Color Plate 7)

AGE: ELEMENTARY SCHOOL AND UP
TIME: HOURS DIVIDED INTO SHORT SESSIONS

This impressive-looking tree is just a step beyond simple pasta-pasting, and a child can do a good part of it alone. The basic tree can be an all-year-round tree or just a winter tree, depending on how it is finished. The winter version can be transformed into a Christmas decoration by the temporary addition of holiday trimmings.

NECESSITIES:

· Pasta shells in sizes ranging from small to giant
· A styrofoam cone (the photographed one is 12" high)
· White glue
· Acrylic paint
· Optional trimmings, such as spray paint, yarn, aluminum foil, dried flowers

STEP-BY-STEP:

1. Put each size shell in a separate flat plate or tray.

2. Put the cone on a piece of wax paper to catch glue drippings and to make it easy to turn the tree while working. Use a turntable if available.

3. Paste shells in a random arrangement to completely cover the styrofoam cone. Start at the bottom of the cone. The first row is more difficult than the rest because the shells have nothing but the styrofoam to adhere to, whereas later rows are also supported by previously applied pasta. For the first row, press pieces against the cone for a few minutes until they set. It is best for an adult or a patient, older child to do this part. Let dry thoroughly before continuing.

4. The rest of the shells will adhere easily enough for a child to manage. But don't give a child the very tiniest shells; an older person should add those afterwards.

5. Don't glue more than two or three touching pieces at one time, lest they start to slide. Keep rotating the cone; by the time the starting place comes around again, the first shells will be sufficiently set and more shells can be added. It is all right to interrupt the work at any time.

6. Be sure to fill in all the empty spaces, even if it is necessary to put shells on top of each other to conceal bare spaces.

7. There is no one "right" way to arrange the shells; a child should not be told where to place pieces. If the arrangement doesn't look right, superimpose other pieces after the child has finished (and after he has left the room!). It is best for an adult or older child to add the tiny shells, anyway.

8. An older child can be shown that there is quite a variation of shapes within each size; one shell may fit better than another, or a particular shell may look more graceful when angled differently. Several pieces can be tested (almost like working a jigsaw puzzle) before selecting one to glue in place. The process becomes a good exercise in shape perception.

9. Paint the entire tree green. A thin acrylic or tempera will get into the crevices better than spray paint. (The photographed tree was painted with acrylic paint, mixed with a blend of gloss and matte medium for a semi-gloss finish.)

10. For a winter tree, spray white paint downward from above in short, close spurts, so that just the upper surfaces of the shells are covered to look like snow.

11. For a summer tree, paste tiny dried flowers in spaces between the shells.

12. Change a winter tree to a Christmas tree in one of the following ways:
   · Roll tiny balls of aluminum foil and push them into crevices between the shells. In addition to foil, metallic gift wrap paper, or colored tissue may be used.
   · Press bits of aluminum foil (about $1'' \times 1\frac{1}{2}''$) into tight balls at intervals along a strand of red yarn. Drape the yarn around the tree.
   · Paste tiny pasta shells about an inch apart on a strand of red yarn. If desired, the shells may be painted. Drape the yarn around the tree.

LASAGNE LOONIES

(*Color Plate 2*)

If children beg for one of those commercial kits of shrinking people, monsters, or other grotesqueries, show them how to make their own weirdos from cooked lasagne. The great fun of these is that there's no illustrated box cover to give away the finished product, so everyone is in for a fantastic surprise.

NECESSITIES:
   · Lasagne
   · Scissors or knife

AGE: ELEMENTARY SCHOOL TO PRE-TEENS
TIME: MINUTES TO PREPARE, PLUS HOURS TO BAKE

   · Aluminum foil coated with cooking oil
   · Cookie sheet
   · Cardboard or plywood backing (optional)

STEP-BY-STEP:
1. Read instructions for modeling pasta, page 87.

2. Cook lasagne according to package directions. Cut pieces into any face or figure shape. A jack-o-lantern or a circle with cutouts for the eyes, nose, and mouth would be easiest. Older

children might want first to make a simple outline pattern of a person or animal as a cutting guide.

3. Lay the cutouts on an oiled piece of aluminum foil on a cookie sheet and put the sheet in the oven with just the pilot light on. Or, if the oven has a warming heat of under 200°, use that temperature. In a couple of hours the heat will have hardened the lasagne into grossly distorted versions of the originals.

4. If desired, paint and glue the pieces to a backing of cardboard or plywood for display.

COOKED PASTA FRAMES

AGE: TEENS AND ADULTS
TIME: MINUTES TO PREPARE; HOURS TO
DAYS TO DRY

PICTURE FRAME

NECESSITIES:
- Spaghetti, 6 or more strands
- Plate or aluminum foil, oiled
- White glue
- Cardboard or other frame
- Metallic silver airplane enamel

STEP-BY-STEP:

1. Figure how much spaghetti is needed. A 5″ diameter frame requires six strands of spaghetti. Each strand curls up into a length of about 2½″, so for a larger frame, measure the circumference to see how many spaghetti strands are needed. Then add half as many more to allow for mishaps.

2. Prepare the spaghetti as described under modeling techniques (page 87).

3. Lightly oil a plate or sheet of aluminum foil of the required circumference, and loop each strand of spaghetti in place to form a circle. The loops can either be curved inward as on the illustrated frame, or outward. Depending on the size of the loops, there should be three or four from each strand.

4. Let them dry; check occasionally to be sure the ends are still curved (they sometimes tend to pull back to their original straight position).

5. When dry, attach with white glue to ready-made frame or cardboard one. Then paint, preferably with a brush. Contrary to expectations, spray paint does not get into the crevices well.

ROPE MIRROR FRAME
(Color Plate 3)

NECESSITIES:
- Fusilli, 8 or more strands
- Oiled aluminum foil
- Metallic gold airplane enamel
- Round mirror, 5¼″ diameter
- Craft cement

STEP-BY-STEP:

1. This actually requires only four strands of fusilli, but prepare eight (according to modeling instructions on page 87) because it's just as easy to assemble two frames at a time and use the components which look best together.

2. Starting about an inch from the end of one strand of fusilli, intertwine another strand into it. At the end, there should be an inch or so left

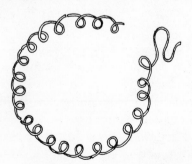

from the second strand. Make a tight connection by intertwining the two leftover ends.

3. Intertwine two more strands evenly from end to end, and knot them into a bow.

4. Make an extra circle, and bow, as in steps 2 and 3.

5. Place the pieces on oiled aluminum foil to dry. It will take at least 24 hours to fully harden. During that time, turn the pieces over occasionally and refine the shapes if necessary. Toward the very end of the drying time, the circles need particular attention.

6. When dry, paint with gold metallic airplane enamel. Do one side at a time and let it dry before turning it over and doing the other side. There is no absolutely safe way of hanging it to permit the entire piece to be painted at once.

7. When completely dry, attach the bow to the circle, concealing the least attractive part. Then attach both to the mirror with a craft cement, formulated for bonding glass and metal. Attach picture hanger on back with the same craft cement.

ON YOUR OWN
• This rope-like trim is an attractive edging for a facial-tissue dispenser. It will require two ropes to equal the perimeter of the tissue box.

JEWELRY

AGE: PRE-TEEN AND UP
TIME: HOURS (DIVIDED INTO MINUTES TO PAINT AND MINUTES TO STRING)

ROTELLE PENDANT NECKLACE
(*Color Plate 5*)

NECESSITIES:
· 6 pieces of rotelle
· 27 pieces of ditalini
· Fluorescent tempera paints
· Yarn or cord about 30″ long
· Thin elastic thread, preferably the same color as rotelle

STEP-BY-STEP:
1. Select two colors of paint and mix with acrylic medium as described in painting techniques (page 88).

2. Paint all rotelle and 9 ditalini one color.

3. Paint the remaining 18 ditalini a second color. (It would be a good idea to make extras of both shapes in case of breakage.)

4. Wrap and tie elastic around rotelle as de-scribed in stringing techniques (page 90).

5. String necklace horizontally with alternating colors, with every fourth bead being a rotelle pendant. Add extra beads at both ends to achieve required length.

6. Tie a knot close to the last bead on each end to prevent beads from moving.

7. Tie the necklace around neck.

ON YOUR OWN
• Colors and number of rotelle can be changed.
• Other types of pendants can be devised by stringing ditalini on spaghetti or fusilli.
• Make original pendants by cutting cooked lasagne into unique shapes.
• Necklace could be strung on a metal chain with clasps from a hobby or jewelry store.

DITALINI NECKLACE AND BRACELET ENSEMBLE
(Color Plate 5)

AGE: TEENS AND ADULTS
TIME: HOURS

NECESSITIES:
- 89 ditalini for the necklace
- 17 ditalini for the bracelet
- Fluorescent tempera paints
- Gold metallic gift wrap cord, or another color cord of similar thickness.

STEP-BY-STEP:

1. Mix the fluorescent temperas with acrylic medium as described in painting techniques (page 88). Paint all ditalini the same color. Paint extras in case of breakage, or in case of later ideas for adding to the ensemble.

2. *Necklace.* Start the necklace with the center pendant. String six ditalini vertically in the middle of a 40″ length of cord. Slide a second cord, 36″ long, through the uppermost ditalini.

3. On each side of center pendant, string a group of four vertical ditalini followed by one horizontal ditalini. Continue until there are eight clusters of vertical ditalini (four on each side of the central pendant). Tie a knot at each end, but do not cut away the cord ends.

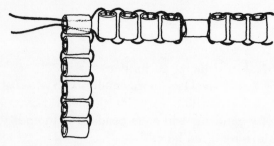

4. Make additional pendants by sliding cord through each horizontal bead and vertically stringing additional beads next to it. Note that the number of beads in each pendant decreases

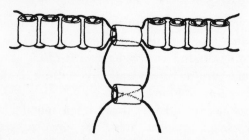

by one as they move away from the center. End each pendant with a knot, but do not cut away the cord ends.

5. At one end of the necklace, tie a second knot a short distance from the first, leaving a loop of about ½″ diameter. At the other end string three ditalini in a row, and knot the ends. Seal all knots on the necklace and pendants with a drop of white glue. When dry, cut off all loose ends. To wear necklace, slip end beads into the cord loop.

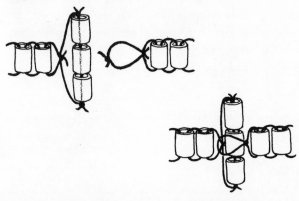

6. *Bracelet.* Using two 14″ cords, string the bracelet with five horizontal ditalini alternating with four clusters of four vertical ditalini. Check the length on the wrist; if necessary, add or delete horizontal ditalini at the ends.

7. Knot a small loop of elasticized thread through the last bead, and secure it with a drop of white glue. At the same time secure the other knots with white glue. When dry, cut away all cord ends. To wear, stretch elastic loop over bead at other end.

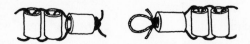

Note: Two finishing methods are shown: a larger one on the necklace, a less conspicuous one on the bracelet. Both are equally effective; if one method is preferred, it may be used on both items.

ON YOUR OWN

Belts can be strung similarly, but larger shapes are needed to add width to the belt. Here are two possibilities:

• For a linked chain effect, interrupt vertical stringing at intervals to put each of the cords through an elbow macaroni. Only a thin stiff thread will curve through the macaroni; use either button and carpet thread, or dental floss. Naturally, the number of ditalini between the pairs of macaroni is optional.

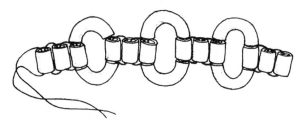

• Diagonally cut, ribbed cylinders can be vertically strung. Because the ends are angled, the appearance of the belt can be controlled by the way each cylinder is turned.

• Belts may be finished the same way as bracelets and necklaces, or the cord ends may be left on for tying.

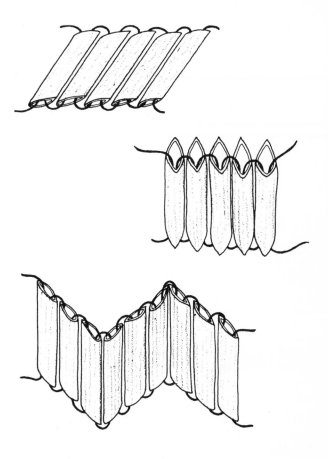

PASTA PILLOW

(Color Plate 7)

AGE: TEENS AND ADULTS
TIME: HOURS

A pasta-stitched motif can be the central decoration of a handsome pillow. Felt is an especially easy fabric to use for a first pillow because it does not ravel and can be very simply stitched to give the effect of a self-corded edge. The stitchery itself can be done directly on the felt or on an easier-to-stitch, looser-woven fabric which will later be appliquéd to the felt. In this case, the central piece is monk's cloth.

NECESSITIES:

· Fabrics
· Yarn
· Crewel-embroidery needle
· Thread (regular sewing and button/carpet)
· Pasta shapes, painted to match, blend, or contrast with the yarns and fabrics
· Embroidery hoop (optional, but advisable)
· Pillow stuffing

STEP-BY-STEP:

1. It is a good idea to paint many more pasta pieces than seem necessary, partly because some may break, but mainly to provide leeway for improvisation while the work is in progress.

2. String macaroni on heavy thread to paint.

3. When dry, push all macaroni close together on the thread so they form a serpentine curve. With a needle, pull both ends of the thread together to the back of the fabric, and knot them.

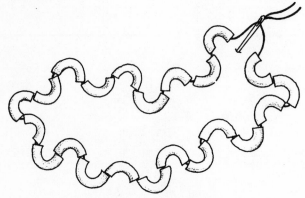

4. Arrange the threaded macaroni into a circle, and use matching sewing thread to catch the center of each macaroni to the fabric.

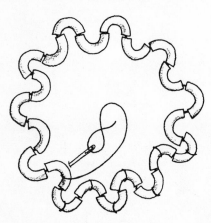

5. Attach pasta wheel with edge stitching.

6. Do lazy daisy stitch from center pasta to each inward curving macaroni.

7. Attach ditalini with matching yarn at outer curve of macaroni.

8. Bring three strands of another color yarn from back to front at a point directly touching one of the ditalini. Curve the three strands around in a circular row of couching, fastening them at each pasta with contrasting yarn. At the end of the circle, bring the three strands of yarn to the back through the original entry hole. Cover the meeting point with the final stitch of yarn.

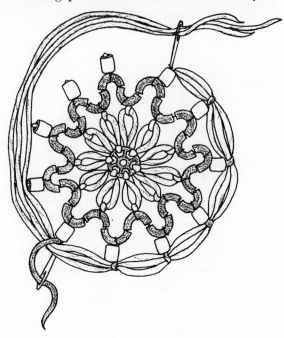

9. Do satin stitches in groups of three.

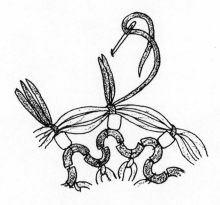

10. Cut excess fabric from around embroidery hoop, and remove hoop.

11. Cut pillow fabric into two squares, 1″ larger than finished size on all 4 sides.

12. Attach circle to front of pillow with satin stitch.

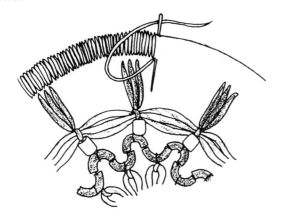

13. Lay front and back of pillow on top of each other, with right sides together. Make a machine row of stitching $\frac{5}{8}$″ from edge, starting just before one corner, and ending just after fourth corner, leaving about a 6″ opening on one side. Trim seams to $\frac{1}{4}$″, except at opening. Cut diagonals away from corners.

14. Turn pillow right side out. Stuff with polyester fiberfill or alternative pillow filling. Fold the seam allowance along the opening to the inside. Stitch $\frac{1}{4}$″ from edge all around pillow for corded knife edge.

ON YOUR OWN

• Stitch directly on the pillow fabric instead of on an appliqué.

• Appliqué a stitched motif onto a previously made pillow or a purchased one.

• A round pillow is made like a square one, leaving a 6″ opening along the circumference through which to insert stuffing. Remember to clip (cut a notch in the seam allowance) so that circle will turn smoothly.

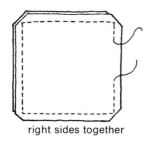

right sides together

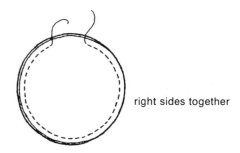

right sides together

Seeds, Peas, Beans, and Barley, Too

For small children, playing with seeds and beans will be similar to playing with pasta, except that most beans and seeds are smaller and smoother than pasta and therefore require better finger control. This means that a child should be able to do the earliest pasting activities suggested in the chapter on pasta before being introduced to beans and seeds. For some children, this will be before they start school; for others, not until early school years.

A good way to start is to give a child a small handful of several kinds of beans and seeds, as different from each other as possible in size, shape, and color. This offers an opportunity to practice recognizing similarities and differences, which is one of the skills needed for learning to read. Suggest that the child put "all these large flat white seeds in this section of the egg carton, and all those round pink beans into that section."

Now provide some paste (see Thick Paste, page 41), and a paper plate or styrofoam tray to paste the seeds and beans onto. As is the case with all new materials, children will place the beans randomly before they try to arrange them into any pattern. Some children find it easy to hold beans and seeds directly in their fingers; others manage better with tweezers. But all should have an opportunity to try both ways because of the slightly different coordination skills involved.

Older children, though, and adults as well, will be ready for a much closer observation of the seeds and beans, which will be helpful for planning designs. Take a really good look at each of the seeds and beans. Notice their minor variations, point them out to children, and explore them together.

Melon and squash seeds have one pointed end and one rounded end. Beans have one side that curves outward and one side that curves inward. The straight or concave side has either a light or a dark spot.

Turn the seeds and beans around in the hand; they may look especially attractive from one particular angle. Perhaps a combination of two beans of contrasting sizes or colors strikes the fancy.

Everyone will have his or her own answers to such questions as: Do beans look better facing in the same direction?

Or do they look better facing each other?

Do beans look better facing in opposite directions?

Does one arrangement, perhaps, work better at the center of a design and another around the edge? This is how designs are developed.

Where to find seeds and beans. Start in the kitchen. There are probably one or more of the following in a cabinet:

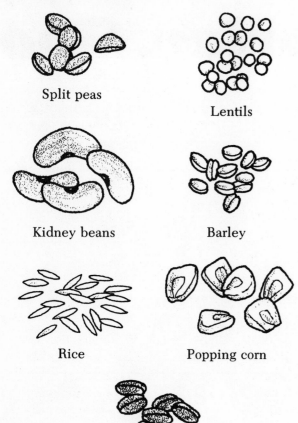

Split peas

Lentils

Kidney beans

Barley

Rice

Popping corn

Coffee beans

Then check the spice shelf for:

Whole cloves

Sesame seeds

Poppy seeds

Caraway seeds

Peppercorns

Supermarkets have a variety of dried beans, seeds, and spices. A good source of unusual seeds and beans is a health food store. If their foods are not pre-packaged, tiny amounts of many different kinds may be bought quite inexpensively.

Get a variety of seeds in one package by buying a bag of mixed birdseed, a box of pickling spices, or the cellophane-wrapped dry soup mixes that have separate layers of beans and grains.

If a gardener, don't throw away leftover planting seeds at the end of the season; save them for crafts. Keep the seeds that develop in the mature flowerheads of sunflowers.

Save pits from olives, peaches, and plums. Also, save seeds from melons, pears, apples, pumpkins, and all kinds of squashes (acorn, Hubbard, butternut).

These techniques are useful when working with seeds:

Preparation. The only seeds that need preparation are those that are removed from fresh foods.

Peach and nectarine pits have an attractive almond-like seed within the hard shell, which needs to be dried out.

Seeds from melons, pumpkins, and winter squash must be washed thoroughly under running water to remove all traces of pulp, then spread in a single layer on a tray to dry.

Drying can be done either in the hot summer sun, or in the oven. Watermelon seeds should remain in a 250° oven for 30–45 minutes. Light-colored seeds have a tendency to brown, so it is safer to leave them in the oven overnight with just the pilot light on.

Glueing. If the seeds are large enough to handle easily, squeeze a dab of white glue directly onto each seed and press it onto the surface.

If the seeds are too small to handle individually, brush glue onto the surface, pour the seeds on, and press them in. When dry, turn the surface over to release the loose seeds into a container. If the background has not been covered satisfactorily, brush another layer of glue onto the surface and press more seeds on.

Embedding. As an alternative to glueing, seeds can be embedded in either tile grout or acrylic modeling paste. This method is useful for making thick and thin beans appear to be at the same surface level.

Another kind of embedding can be done after glueing, if the seeds have been glued onto a surface with a higher framed edge. Clear casting resin can be poured over the seeds up to the level of the frame so that the top surface will be completely flat. This method is attractive for paperweights.

Finishing. Select products to finish seeds projects from the following list:

Polyurethane varnish gives the most attractive gloss finish.

Acrylic gloss medium is a close second, and would be the preferred finish for children to use.

Acrylic gel is a thicker medium and is useful for holding irregularly-shaped seeds in place if the glued surface is not flat enough to come into good contact with the background.

Acrylic matte varnish is good for a low-luster finish.

Clear polyester casting resin may be either brushed on or poured on to completely cover the seeds. It is the shiniest finish.

(Spray plastics are not recommended because they do not effectively secure the smaller seeds in place.)

PROJECTS

SAMPLER PLAQUE
(Color Plate 3)

AGE: PRE-TEENS AND UP
TIME: MINUTES TO HOURS

Circles of about 3″ diameter are a convenient size for experimental samplers. If using the insides of matching jar lids or a set of discarded coasters, or some other uniform circles, a wall hanging can be made from the samplers that turn out best.

Perhaps everyone in the family would like to make one or two; there might then be enough for a really large wall hanging. Of if some kitchen cabinets are unadorned, do the samplers on a larger background—coffee can lids, for example —and glue one circle in the center of each cabinet door.

If some degree of uniformity is desired, select one design format to be used on all the samplers, such as:

· A central flower-like motif
· A series of concentric circles
· Geometric divisions of the circle into quarters or sixths

If the whole family is participating, maybe everyone would rather work out his or her own ideas.

NECESSITIES:
- Circle backgrounds
- White glue
- Assorted beans and seeds
- One of the finishes listed on page 103.

STEP-BY-STEP:

1. Paste seeds and nuts onto the background according to the instructions under glueing techniques on page 103. First do the center, then the outer edge. While selecting beans or seeds for the edge, put aside one or two particularly large ones and the same number of especially small ones. The odd sizes may be needed to make the circle meet perfectly at the end.

2. After the center and edge have dried, sprinkle the middle areas with something smaller, flatter, and of contrasting color. Sometimes, in order to get a special background color, it may be necessary to cheat slightly by sprinkling on such non-beans as:
- Paprika
- Mustard powder or curry powder
- Coffee grounds (used ones are all right if spread to dry thoroughly in the sun or a warm oven)

The photographed plaques are made with the following seeds and beans (starting from the center of each circle):

LEFT PLAQUE

Top—Pea beans, red kidney beans, barley, black turtle soup beans

Middle—Green split pea, cantaloupe seeds, caraway seeds, green split peas

Bottom—Clove head, zucchini seeds, poppy seeds, pink beans

RIGHT PLAQUE

Top—Yellow split pea, cantaloupe seeds on watermelon seeds, paprika, lima beans

Middle—Black turtle soup beans, rye seeds, red lentils, watermelon seeds

Bottom—Yellow split pea, poppy seeds, lima beans, mustard seeds, black turtle soup beans

3. When dry, coat the samplers with the selected finish.

ON YOUR OWN

•To make samplers into a wall plaque, glue them onto one or more wood or Formica panels. Or, line them up on a long strip of wood for horizontal or vertical display.

•To make samplers into paperweights, glue the seeds inside jar lids and cover with clear casting resin. This product is a variation of epoxy finish which is intended for molds and other thick applications. It consists of a resin into which a few drops of hardener must be mixed before use. It has harmful vapors and should only be used by adults or mature teens. When the resin has hardened, paste felt-textured, self-sticking contact paper on bottom (that is, the outside of the lid). (Color Plate 6)

MOSAIC PICTURES

NECESSITIES:
- Plywood or wood fiberboard, framed
- Assorted seeds and beans
- White glue
- Rug yarn, black or other dark color
- Polyurethane varnish

STEP-BY-STEP:

1. Make a line drawing picture on the background.

2. Squeeze glue along a section of the line at a time, and press rug yarn onto it. Avoid cutting the yarn unless absolutely necessary; it is better to shape it by overlapping.

wrong

right

3. If the yarn *must* be cut, cover the cut end with the piece it meets.

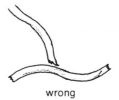

wrong

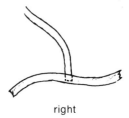

right

4. Select seeds and beans whose color and texture are appropriate for each part of the picture. Brush glue onto one area at a time, and place or sprinkle the appropriate seeds onto the background.

5. When the entire picture is completely dry, an adult should varnish it.

BOOKENDS
(*Color Plate 6*)

Seeds can cover the most mundane items and give them new life. These ordinary metal bookends look brand new, covered with ornamental corn.

NECESSITIES:
- Ornamental corn (or other seeds or beans)
- White glue
- Metal bookends
- Acrylic gel

AGE: TEENS AND ADULTS
TIME: HOURS (INCLUDING INTERVALS FOR DRYING)

STEP-BY-STEP:

1. To make an organized design with ornamental corn, separate the kernels according to color.

2. Attach the kernels with white glue, starting at the edges, and letting each row slightly overlap the preceding one. Let each row dry slightly before starting the next.

3. When dry, coat with acrylic gel.

FLOWERPOTS
(*Color Plate 6*)

Even those plastic pots that little plants from the 5&10 come in can be given a new look.

NECESSITIES:
- Plastic flower pots
- Acrylic paint (optional)
- White glue
- Assorted seeds and beans
- Epoxy resin finish

STEP-BY-STEP:

1. Thoroughly wash and dry each flowerpot. If it is white, paint the outside and the rim inside with a dark color of acrylic paint, which will be less conspicuous when spaces show through between the seeds.

AGE: PRE-TEENS AND UP
TIME: HOURS (INCLUDING INTERVALS FOR DRYING)

2. Glue on seeds. Because the flowerpots are curved, only a few seeds or beans can be glued on at a time; more would slide off.

One of the illustrated pots was done with green split peas and pinto beans. The other was done with red kidney beans and navy beans.

3. When dry, coat with epoxy resin to weatherproof the pots for outdoor use.

ON YOUR OWN
- Other ordinary items that can be enhanced with an encrustation of beans are dime-store mirrors with handles, picture frames, and empty cans, jars, or bottles.
- Paste samples of the kind of beans within onto canisters.

MELON SEED PENDANT NECKLACE

AGE: TEENS AND ADULTS
TIME: HOURS

(*Color Plate 4*)

The carefully placed cantaloupe seeds are very effective on this pendant, particularly since they can also be used for the necklace part. Other seeds that don't require as careful placement could be equally well used for a pendant, but they could not be strung for the necklace.

NECESSITIES:
- Seeds from one cantaloupe, prepared as described on page 102
- Basil seeds (or poppy seeds)
- White glue
- Plastic can lid (this one is 2¾″ in diameter)
- Acrylic matte varnish
- Needle and thread

STEP-BY-STEP:

1. Insert doubled strand of thread through plastic lid as illustrated. About 20″ should extend from lid at each end.

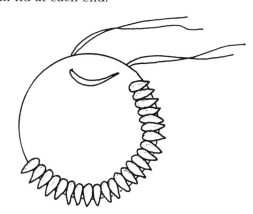

2. Glue a circle of cantaloupe seeds around the circumference of the lid. The sharp points should be turned outward, and they should extend slightly beyond the edge of the lid.

3. When the first row is partly dry, glue on the second row, slightly overlapping the first. This pendant was continued until there were five rows of seeds. A larger or smaller circle might need proportionately more or fewer rows.

4. Glue small black seeds in the center. The ones used for the photographed necklace are basil seeds, which are extremely black. If they are unavailable, poppy seeds are an adequate substitute. In order to build up the height in the center, glue on a second layer of seeds after the first is dry.

5. Glue a flat row of cantalope seeds around the side to cover the edge of the lid.

6. With a very thin sharp needle, string cantaloupe seeds on 15″ of the thread on each side of the pendant. Knot the thread ends tightly. Hide the thread ends by threading each end through seeds on the opposite side as far as the thread can go, then cut.

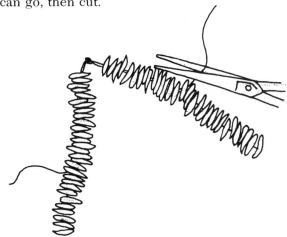

7. The center was coated with acrylic matte varnish. Since there is no appropriate way of sealing the seeds that are strung on the necklace, the cantaloupe seeds on the pendant were also left untreated so they would not look different.

ON YOUR OWN

• Cantaloupe seeds are also attractive with their narrow end uppermost. It is impossible to paste them that way, but they can be embedded in acrylic modeling paste in a small plastic jar lid, like the photographed one, which was then sealed with acrylic gel. This method is suitable for making a belt buckle, a pin, or a paperweight. (Color Plate 4)

• A lovely, but more time-consuming, way to string cantaloupe seeds is on a double thread. Be sure to align the seeds so that all the pointed ends face in the same direction.

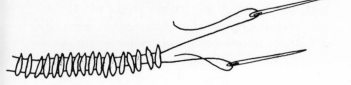

• Because cantaloupe seeds can be threaded so easily, they can be used in stitchery. Read the section on pasta stitchery (pages 90–91) for ideas.

Particular colors and shapes of seeds and beans were suggested for the preceding projects. Here are a few things that can be done with whatever kinds are left.

NAMEPLATE

A child's name is one of his or her most important possessions; it establishes unique identity within the family and produces an important self-image. That is why children are so proud when they have learned to write their names!

Children who can print their names can make their very own name plaque for their desk or the door.

NECESSITIES:
· A block of wood
· Two kinds of seeds or beans that contrast well
· A pencil
· Acrylic gel

AGE: ELEMENTARY SCHOOL AND PRE-TEENS
TIME: MINUTES

STEP-BY-STEP:
1. Have the child print his or her name in pencil on the wood.
2. Glue the larger seeds onto the pencil lines and let them dry.
3. Glue the other seeds in the remaining areas.
4. When dry, brush acrylic gel over all.

ON YOUR OWN
• Make a large family nameplate for the front door or for the mailbox.

BEANBAGS

Every child should have a couple of beanbags for learning to catch, for learning to throw, for learning to aim well, and for learning to juggle.

NECESSITIES:
· Two pieces of sturdy fabric for each 4–5″ squares or circles are the most useful.
· Medium-size beans

AGE: ELEMENTARY SCHOOL AND UP (TO MAKE); PRESCHOOL AND ELEMENTARY SCHOOL (TO USE)
TIME: MINUTES

STEP-BY-STEP:
1. Stitch two pieces of fabric together, right sides facing, leaving about $2\frac{1}{2}$″ unstitched. Machine-stitching is preferable, but if a child

who doesn't yet use the sewing machine is making the bag, short running stitches will be all right.

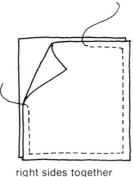

right sides together

2. Turn right side out, fill with beans, then close the opening with slip stitches. For reinforcement, a row of machine stitches can be put close to the edge, or blanket stitches (see page 91) can be hand-sewn.

ON YOUR OWN
• Decorative beanbags can be made of felt or other attractive fabrics, shaped to look like butterflies or owls or fruits. They are appealing projects for novices at fancy stitchery, but are not as practical for play.

LAYERED BEANS

AGE: ADULTS
TIME: MINUTES

Layered sand is ubiquitous by now, but layered beans are something else! In a tall narrow jar they look very handsome. Plan an attractive sequence of colors and shapes. Put larger beans on top of smaller ones, for this reason: smaller ones will slip down between large ones, making an irregular dividing line; but larger ones cannot slip between smaller ones.

If the composition absolutely requires smaller beans on top of larger ones, separate the layers with a circle of cardboard slightly smaller than the jar circumference.

To save on the number of beans used, hide an inner core of cardboard or foil in the center of the jar and pour the seeds around it.

ON YOUR OWN
• For other seed projects, see the seed mosaic pendants and plaques in the chapter on Kitchen Clays (page 20, 23, and 24).

Egg Art and Craft

Eggs are so simple in shape and color that they lend themselves to nearly every imaginable craft technique: painting, printing, dyeing, marbleizing, collage, découpage, weaving, and more!

Most paints and dyes look more brilliant on raw eggshells than on cooked eggshells; therefore, most projects begin with blowing out the contents of the shells in order to keep the shells intact but not waste the food within.

Because the empty shells are too fragile and too confining an area for young children to work on, egg decorating is not especially recommended for those under eight or nine. On the other hand, if a family egg-decorating project is going on, don't leave a younger child out of it; provide hardboiled eggs instead. Here are some of the things a young child can do with them:

- Paint the shells with tempera.
- Apply stick-ons from the stationery store, such as notebook reinforcements, colored metallic stars, self-sticking shapes and pictures.
- Print patterns by pressing a fingertip, sponge, or pencil eraser onto a stamp pad and then onto the eggshell. Or print with tempera paints, as described in the chapter on potato printing (page 59).

These eggs, of course, will be eaten because no one wants to waste hardboiled eggs, and anyway, young children don't especially care about saving their finished creations for more than one or two days.

Young children and pre-teens often like to make caricature faces on eggs. Tempera paints or felt-tip markers are fine for this. Provide a boxful of collage materials for adding features, such as sequins for eyes, yarn for hair, etc. No purpose is served in showing a child what kind of faces to copy. A child who is interested will instinctively create his or her own; if not, examples won't lure him into the activity. Use hardboiled eggs for a fun activity; use blown eggshells for a collection of faces to be on display.

You might not want to decorate more than one or two eggs with the same technique, but since the preliminaries are the same for all egg-decorating, it is much simpler to prepare at least a dozen eggs at once. Children, even teens, may not have the patience for the preparation, so an adult might prefer to do it as a solitary activity. After preparing them, you can store the shells in the original egg carton until time to decorate them.

Basic Procedure

Step 1 — *Blowing the eggs.* If you've never done this before, allow about five minutes for the first egg; the rest will go faster.

NECESSITIES:
- Long sharp-pointed needle or hat pin
- Small bowl or custard cup for contents of one egg at a time
- Large bowl for accumulating all the egg contents
- Bowl of water for rinsing empty shells

STEP-BY-STEP:

1. Let the eggs reach room temperature; cold ones are difficult to blow.

2. Hold the point of the needle or pin on the narrow tip of the egg with one hand. With a knife handle or similar utensil in the other hand, gently tap the needle or pin until it pierces the egg shell. Push it about halfway into the egg, and then remove it.

3. Repeat the procedure on the large end of the

egg. Enlarge this second hole to about $\frac{1}{8}''$ or $\frac{1}{4}''$ diameter by gently breaking off tiny pieces of shell with the needle tip. If some cracks develop around the hole, cover them later with ribbon or some other decorative element.

Another method of enlarging the hole is by gently twisting the sharp, narrow blade of embroidery scissors in the hole. This gives a smooth round hole, but sometimes eggshell dust can fall into the opening and cause a gritty omelet. Try it, though, to see if this method seems preferable.

4. Now jab the needle all the way into the hole and move it around to break the membrane covering the yolk. Hold the egg with a finger covering each hole, and shake as hard as possible to mix the contents.

5. Wipe mouth dry, hold the egg with the small opening against the lips, and blow hard until the contents are expelled into the small bowl. If the egg is all right (no shell or blood spots), transfer it into the larger bowl.

6. To clean the inside of the shell, submerge the large hole in a bowl of water, and suck hard on the small hole to bring water into the shell. Shake the egg, then blow out the water. Repeat a second time, rinse the outside of the shell, and lay the egg on a tray or paper towels to dry.

When all the shells are dry, you will be ready to begin the second part of the preparation.

Meanwhile, get the egg contents back into the refrigerator promptly, and be sure to use them within a day for omelets, custard, cake, or French toast. Or freeze them. (For each $\frac{1}{2}$ cup—about 6 eggs—add either $\frac{3}{4}$ teaspoon sugar *or* $\frac{1}{4}$ teaspoon salt, depending on whether they will later be used for baking or general cooking. Stir. Divide into as many ice cube tray sections as there are eggs. When frozen, the cubes may be packed together in a plastic bag; each cube equals one egg.)

Step 2—*Priming the eggshell.* Paint the eggshells with a coat of diluted white glue to give them a smooth finish and strengthen them somewhat. Note: it does *not* make the shells unbreakable!

- White glue
- Water
- Mixing bowl
- Soft-haired brush about $\frac{1}{2}''$ wide
- Bamboo skewers or party toothpicks 4–5" long (one for each egg)
- Strong corrugated carton around which to prop skewered eggshells (an alternative would be lumps of non-hardening plastic clay)

STEP-BY-STEP:

1. Dilute the glue with about $\frac{1}{3}$ as much water. The consistency should be like light cream, just loose enough to flow smoothly from the brush.

2. Arrange shells on skewers as shown.

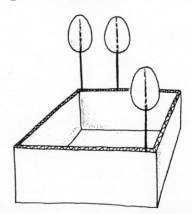

An alternative to a corrugated cardboard box would be to stick the skewers into lumps of non-hardening plastic clay. These methods make it possible to paint the entire egg at once and allow it to dry with all sides exposed to the air.

3. Hold the egg at the narrow end and paint the other half with diluted glue. Then slip the

egg, painted side down, onto the skewer. With one finger tip gently resting on top of the egg, paint the rest of the egg with diluted glue.

Finally, remove the finger and paint over the little hole.

4. Before the glue is thoroughly dry, check the bottom; if a bead of glue has accumulated, wipe it off with the brush. Be sure not to let the glue harden on the brush. Keep the bristles in water when not in use, and wash it in soapy warm water immediately after finishing.

Step 3 — Base coat of paint (optional). If the egg is to be some other color than white, apply a base coat with any of the following paints:

Tempera, which is the only recommended paint for younger children.

Acrylic paints, for older children and adults.

Model airplane paints, for older children and adults. The colors are brilliantly glossy. The metallics (gold, silver, and copper) are especially beautiful.

Brush on paints in the same manner as the method used to brush on the diluted glue.

Spray paints, for teens and adults only.

Spray painting requires that the egg be suspended in a shielded area.

NECESSITIES:
- Carton
- Thread (if this is the thread the finished egg will hang by, it should match the spray paint)
- Half toothpick
- White glue
- Dowel or pencil

STEP-BY-STEP:

1. Prepare the egg for hanging. Put a dab of glue on the middle of the toothpick half, and wrap the end of the thread around it several

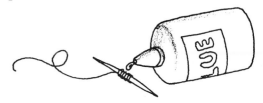

times. Secure with another dab of glue, smooth it down, and let dry. When dry, push the toothpick all the way into the larger hole and then pull the thread so that the toothpick becomes wedged inside the egg crosswise. Tie the loose end of the thread to a dowel or pencil. The distance between eggshell and dowel should be about 6″.

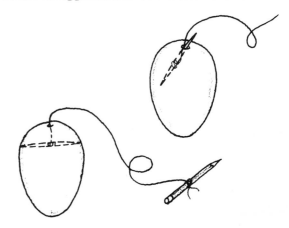

2. Prepare the carton. If carton has top flaps, cut off one of them. Turn carton on side with open end facing you and the side with the missing flap on top. Cut hole in top only large enough for the

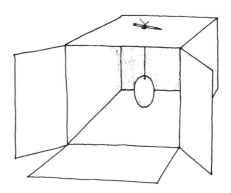

dowel to pass through. Slip dowel through the hole from the inside of the carton; lay the dowel crosswise on the hole so that the egg is suspended.

3. Spray, following spray can instructions. Cover the working area under the carton with newspapers in case the spray drifts. Turn the dowel as necessary to be sure the paint is reaching all parts of the eggshell.

4. Suspend eggshells to dry. A setup like this will provide space to hang a number of eggs to dry simultaneously. Produce cartons are best because they already have six holes in the bottom. Turn bottom end to top, cut away one side, and protect surface from drips with newspapers.

5. Plan for the display of your eggs. If they are to be hung, try to incorporate the hanging device into the design. Some will need to be done before decorating. These are some possibilities:
• Hanging by a thread. Insert the thread as described in the section on spray painting. The thread hole can be covered later with a bead or a pasted trim.
• Hanging by yarn. Thread yarn onto needle

longer than egg length (or make a needle by twisting a thin wire around the yarn). Draw yarn into bottom of egg and out through the top. Remove needle, and knot yarn at top (optional) and at bottom (essential). A group of eggs can be strung together in this way.

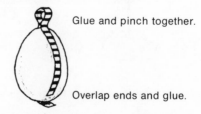

Glue and pinch together.

Overlap ends and glue.

• Loop of ribbon. This will require a ribbon around the entire egg. For maximum strength, the cut part should be on bottom, not on top where the loop is.
• A bow. For maximum strength, the bow should be tied onto a ribbon or yarn that is wrapped around the egg, rather than just glued onto the top.

Eggs can also be displayed on a stand. The stand can be a specially designed egg stand, a curtain ring, an upside-down bottle cap, or something improvised from an egg carton section. This requires no special preparation, except to plan a design that doesn't require a bottom decoration. It is an excellent way to display otherwise attractive eggs which have imperfect holes or other slight damages at one end.

The eggs are now ready to be decorated.

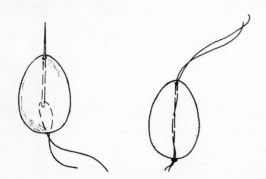

BERIBBONED GLITTER EGG

(*Color Plate 8*)

AGE: PRE-TEEN AND UP
TIME: MINUTES

NECESSITIES:
- One blown eggshell, primed
- Small package of glitter (from 5&10 or hobby store)
- One-half yard of $\frac{3}{8}''$ ribbon
- White glue

STEP-BY-STEP:

1. Draw quadrant lines lightly in pencil.
2. Brush glue on one section at a time, not going closer than $\frac{1}{8}''$ to the line. Roll and press the egg into glitter spread on a sheet of paper.

3. Repeat until entire egg, except the quadrant lines, is covered. Replace on skewer until dry.

4. When dry, wrap and glue a length of ribbon around the egg, beginning and ending at the bottom. When that is dry, wrap and glue a second length of ribbon also beginning and ending at the bottom, but leaving a loop on top if it is to be hung.

ON YOUR OWN
- Use multicolor glitter.
- Wrap one ribbon vertically and one horizontally, with a bow where they intersect.
- Instead of glitter, use colored terrarium sand. For a picture or design, draw the outlines on the egg with pencil. Cover all areas with glue that are to be the same color; roll in selected color of sand, which will stick only to the glue. When dry, repeat for the next color. Spray finished egg with clear plastic.

EMBOSSED METALLIC EGG

(*Color Plate 8*)

AGE: PRE-TEEN AND UP
TIME: MINUTES

This elegant egg is deceptively simple to do.

NECESSITIES:
- One blown eggshell, primed
- Metallic silver model airplane paint
- Silver foil doilies
- White glue
- Acrylic matte varnish

STEP-BY-STEP:

1. Paint an egg with a base coat of metallic silver airplane paint.
2. Cut sections from the foil doilies. They can be cut apart selectively into an infinite number of variations. This makes doilies an excellent medium for a group of children working together, or for a family project, because everyone's

individual perception will almost guarantee that all the designs will be different; yet, because they all use the same basic material, there will be a unity that relates them. Have plenty of doilies on hand; sometimes it takes considerable experimentation to find the perfect combination.

On the photographed egg, each of the little flower patterns is a separate piece. One of them is also pasted at the top and at the bottom to cover the blowing holes.

3. Attach the doily pieces to the egg with a dab of white glue on the back of the doily; press it against the egg for a moment. When the glue has dried, protect the egg with a coat of acrylic matte varnish.

MEDALLIONED BLACK EGG
(*Color Plate 8*)

This is actually a variation of the Embossed Metallic Egg, but it shows how different the effect is when the background *contrasts* with, rather than *matches,* the foil.

NECESSITIES:
   · One blown eggshell, primed
   · Black spray paint or black acrylic paint
   · Silver foil doilies
   · White glue
   · Acrylic matte varnish

In order to make the circular pattern from the doily conform to the oval shape of the egg, cut the loop design and remove several sections of it until it can be fitted attractively on the egg.

ON YOUR OWN
   • Try different monochrome combinations of egg and doily: gold on gold, white on white, or paint egg and doily the same color.
   • Try bright-colored eggs with white doily cutouts.

SEQUINED EGGS
(*Color Plate 8*)

Packages of sequins, either all the same, or with varied shapes and colors, provide more freedom than glitter does in designing a sparkling egg. The sequins conform better to the shape of the egg if they are applied upside-down (that is, with the convex side facing upward).

NECESSITIES:
   · One blown eggshell, primed
   · Sequins
   · Tweezers (optional)
   · White glue
   · Clear plastic spray

1. Smear white glue on a piece of scrap paper. Dip the sequins in it, and press onto the eggshell. If the sequins are very small, tweezers may be helpful.

Instead of this,

put convex side facing upward.

2. To hide the top blowing hole, thread the hanging cord through a sequin, dab glue around the hole, and press the sequin into it. Cover the bottom hole with another sequin.

3. When glue is dry, spray with clear plastic. (The surface is too irregular to apply a brushed-on finish.)

ON YOUR OWN
- Use different background colors.
- Arrange the sequins in a pattern or design.

DOTTY EGGS
(*Color Plate 8*)

AGE: PRE-TEEN AND UP
TIME: MINUTES

The egg with the dots and the one with dots and stripes were done with the self-adhesive products available in stationery stores which carry office supplies. Both the "coding dots" and the "chart tape" come in a variety of colors and sizes.

ON YOUR OWN
- Keep your eyes open for unusual self-adhesive shapes to paste on eggs. For instance:
  · Play shapes, in toy or art stores
  · Gift-wrap tapes, where holiday supplies are sold
  · Contact vinyl papers, in hardware stores
  · Colored cellophane and/or plastic tape, in hardware stores
- Although self-adhesives are easiest to use, there is an even wider variety of non-adhesives suitable for pasting onto eggs. Any paper, any fabric, and many chunky things can be pasted onto eggshells. Small pieces can be pasted in a patchwork arrangement.
- A home-made substitute for "coding dots" can be made with a hole puncher and any colored paper, even patterned paper from magazine illustrations. Punching holes is great fun (and good hand and finger exercise!) for children as young as four.

TISSUE COLLAGE EGG
(*Color Plate 8*)

Multiple layers of tissue paper and acrylic medium result in a glowing, shimmering egg. This is an easy one-step technique because it can be done on unprimed eggshells and does not require a separate finish afterwards.

NECESSITIES:
- One blown eggshell, unprimed
- Colored tissue papers in two to four colors
- Acrylic gloss medium
- Soft-haired brush ½″ wide
- Small pan of water (to dip brush into occasionally, when medium accumulates too thickly on bristles)

STEP-BY-STEP:
1. Tear tissue papers into strips or other shapes. Unless a random design is planned, keep each color separate.
2. Holding the egg at the narrow end, brush medium on a small section near the large hole. Cover it with tissue, and brush on some more medium to hold it.
3. Continue the same procedure on adjacent sections, alternately brushing medium and covering with tissue. When the lower half of the egg is covered, slip it onto the skewer and finish the top.
4. Tissue colors tend to bleed, wrinkled areas become darker, and superimposed colors blend, so that the final result is a far more varied mix of colors than the original tissues. For extra brilliance, leave some areas white.
5. While the egg is drying, periodically check the bottom and wipe away any beads of medium that accumulate.

ON YOUR OWN
- For a good family project select a color scheme and supply some tissue paper. Everyone is likely to tear out different shapes and apply them differently, so the result will be a set of unique, but color-related, eggs, which will make a nice group display.
- Tissue collage eggs can be used for miniature surprise gifts. Use eggs that are cracked in half fairly neatly. Remove the inner membrane, and wash and dry the shells. Put a little trinket (or how about a fortune?) in each. Seal the shell closed with strips of white tissue and medium around the crack. Let dry before proceeding with the rest of the collaging.

DÉCOUPAGE EGG
(*Color Plate 8*)

Découpage is the centuries-old art of covering pasted-on papers with twenty or more coats of varnish or lacquer until the pattern appears to be embedded in the background.

Traditional découpage is strictly for adults, and purists would sneer at any shortcuts. However, this deceptive découpage project could help someone decide whether the technique and the results warrant investing the time and effort to take it up seriously. The photographed egg looks like fine porcelain with a painted pattern.

NECESSITIES:
- One blown eggshell, either primed or unprimed
- Very tiny pictures carefully cut out (seed catalogs are a good source)
- Acrylic gloss medium

- Soft-haired brush about ½″ wide
- Pan of water to rest brush in
- Disposable pan for diluting medium (section of styrofoam egg carton is fine)
- Very fine steel wool (size 0000)

STEP-BY-STEP:

1. Dilute gloss medium with about half as much water; stir.

2. If the egg has not been primed, prime it now with a coat of diluted medium, and let dry. Check the bottom and wipe off any bead of medium that accumulates.

3. Coat the primed egg with diluted gloss medium, and before it dries press the cut-outs onto the surface.

4. Let dry. Then apply at least three more coats of medium, allowing drying time of at least 15–30 minutes between the coats. (Drying time of later coats is longer than for earlier coats.) Lightly touch the bottom to test for dryness each time; that's the part that dries last. Change the direction of brush strokes with each coat, first horizontal, then vertical.

5. Run a fingernail over the pasted-on pictures. If you can still feel the edge, keep applying additional coats of medium until the entire surface feels smooth to the fingernail. Then rub steel wool lightly in circles to make the surface even smoother.

6. Rinse under running water to make sure no steel wool has adhered. Then finish with one final coat of medium.

Découpage is also done on wood, metal, and ceramic. To learn more about this art, one of the finest books is *Découpage Old and New*, by Elyse Sommer (New York: Watson-Guptill, 1971).

MOSAIC EGGS

(*Color Plate 8*)

AGE: TEENS AND ADULTS
TIME: MINUTES TO HOURS

We've now pasted everything onto eggshells except *other* eggshells! That's next.

NECESSITIES:

- One blown eggshell, primed and painted a solid color
- Broken eggshells (saved from earlier accidents)
- White glue
- Soft-haired brush, about ½″ wide
- Tweezers
- Acrylic matte varnish

STEP-BY-STEP:

1. Break the broken eggshells into even smaller mosaic-like pieces of dimensions between ⅛″ and ½″. Keep the larger and smaller ones separate.

2. Brush the egg with glue, a small area at a time, and press the shell pieces onto it. Tweezers

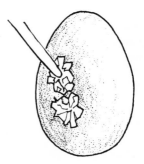

will be helpful with the tiniest pieces. Leave just a very narrow space between the mosaic pieces, and try to graduate the size of the pieces to enhance the design. Be sure to cover the blowing holes.

3. When dry, finish with a coat of acrylic matte varnish.

ON YOUR OWN
• Use a colored eggshell for the mosaic pieces — or several different colors.
• Use a white background egg and black mosaic pieces, or vice versa.

• Another kind of mosaic can be done by painting or dyeing eggshells, crushing them, and using the shell bits the same way as glitter in Glitter Eggs, page 115.
• Eggshell mosaics can be applied to objects other than eggs. See instructions for Eggshell Mosaic Plate, page 123.

CAGED EGGS
(*Color Plate 8*)

AGE: TEENS AND ADULTS
TIME: MINUTES (WITH INTERVALS FOR DRYING)

This is one of many ways to wrap eggs with yarn. The simplest way, one continuous spiral of yarn, pushed into place on a glue-covered egg, can be done by children. But caged eggs require a steady hand and some finger dexterity, and are probably best saved for teen-agers and adults.

NECESSITIES:
· 2 blown eggshells, primed (and, if desired, painted a solid color)
· 4 pieces of yarn, 30″ long
· 1 piece of yarn 10″ long
· White glue

STEP-BY-STEP:
1. Lay the four long pieces of yarn together, and tie the shorter piece around the midpoint.

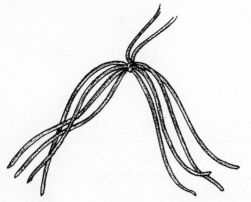

Pick it up by the knot; the short piece will be the hanging cord, and there are now eight lengths of yarn radiating from the knot.

2. Smear a ½″ circle of glue around the top of one egg, and press the center knot against it. Holding the egg in place, arrange the yarn in equidistant spokes and hold in place until the glue starts to harden. Put aside to finish drying.

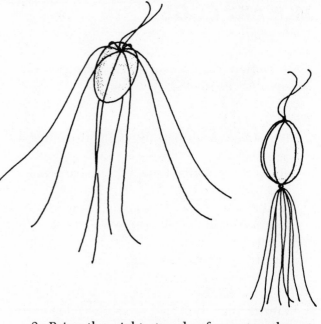

3. Bring the eight strands of yarn together at the bottom of the egg, while trying to keep them still equally spaced around the middle of the

egg. Tie the yarn into a knot close to the bottom of the egg. Dab glue under and around the knot, and press the yarn adjacent to the knot into place, equally spaced around the knot.

4. When dry repeat with second egg. The tassel which forms on bottom can be left plain, braided, or macraméd.

ON YOUR OWN
• Any number of eggs can be used, with the length of the yarn strands adjusted accordingly.
• Caged eggs can be considered a warped loom.

Yarn can be woven around the egg. Note that because there is an even number of warp threads, each warp will always be under or over the weft. To remedy this, use *two* wefts. After the first has been woven (not too closely) in a spiral from top to bottom, weave the second one in between, reversing the over-and-under pattern.
• Other wrappings besides yarn can be used: raffia, embroidery floss, shiny macramé cord, twisted crepe paper or tissue paper, strings of Indian beads or tiny pearls.

MARBLEIZED EGGS
(*Color Plate 8*)

AGE: TEENS AND ADULTS
TIME: MINUTES TO MAKE, DAYS TO DRY

This is one of the most beautiful techniques, always with unpredictable results. Allow plenty of time because it's so much fun that after all the eggs are finished, it's exciting to try the technique on paper, styrofoam cups and trays, fabric, wood, and who knows what else! It's a little messy, though (particularly the cleanup), so save this for teens and adults.

NECESSITIES:
· Three colors of artists' oil paint. Buy the smallest size tubes, either primary colors (red, yellow, and blue), or related shades (e.g. red, orange, and magenta)
· Turpentine or paint thinner, for thinning paints and for cleaning up
· Unprimed eggshells (because the paint adheres better) on hanging threads
· Disposable partitioned tray for mixing paints (styrofoam egg carton or TV dinner tray)
· Three tiny plastic spoons (such as come with granulated sugar substitutes). Ordinary plastic spoons can also be used.

· Container deep enough to hold egg (disposable foil meat loaf pan, or cottage cheese container)
· Toothpick or discardable plastic fork
· Clear plastic spray

STEP-BY-STEP:
1. Squeeze about 1½ teaspoon of each color paint into a separate section of the mixing tray. Add turpentine gradually while stirring with spoon until the paint is liquid.

2. Fill the deep container with water. Using a separate spoon for each color paint, lay a drop gently on the surface of the water in several places. Draw a toothpick or fork tines across the surface until the streaks of color interweave with each other. The colors will now adhere to anything that touches the surface.

3. Roll an egg, attached to a string, across the top of the liquid until the marbleized pattern covers it. Or quickly submerge the entire egg (it's bouyant, so it must be pushed down with a fork), and twist it by the string as it rises.

4. Hang the egg to dry the same way as spray-

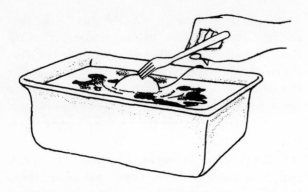

painted eggs (page 114). Oil paints are very slow-drying. Allow at least one day for thin colors, two days or more for thicker colors.

5. When dry, protect the eggs with a clear plastic spray.

ON YOUR OWN

• The more paint there is on the surface of the water, the thicker and deeper the colors will be. As the paint is taken up on the eggshells, the remaining colors become more spotted and delicate. Which to use is a matter of taste. If the colors get too pale, add a few more drops of each color. To produce the lighter colors, make paint additions very sparingly, and marbleize something else before dipping the eggs.

• Here are some other items that can be marbleized with leftover paint:
  · Styrofoam cups and trays
  · Paper, either smooth typing paper or rice paper; try any others that are available and perhaps make a new discovery!
  · Wood
  · Fabric, which will then be washable

• For best results in marbleizing large pieces, a roasting pan would be necessary for a big enough paint surface. Marbleized paper is handsome for covering books, note pads, and gift boxes. (See instructions for these items in the chapter on potato printing, pages 78 and 79.)

FOOD COLORING MARBLEIZED EGGS
AGE: ELEMENTARY SCHOOL AND UP
TIME: MINUTES

Although the results are not as dramatic as with the oil paints, the cleanup is easier.

NECESSITIES:
  · One or more unprimed eggshells
  · Liquid food coloring
  · Clear plastic spray (to be used by adult)

STEP-BY-STEP:

1. An optional first step is to tint the eggs in a diluted mixture of food color and water according to the package instructions.

2. After the egg is dry, let one drop of food color spill onto it directly from the bottle. Holding the egg at top and bottom, quickly turn the egg around and blow on the liquid in order to control the flow of the color.

3. When it is partly dry, add a drop of another color, and repeat the blowing and turning. Colors will blend on wet areas and will form hard edges on dry areas. Keep repeating until you like the effect.

4. An adult will have to spray this with a clear plastic sealer.

PSEUDO-PYSANKY EGG

(*Color Plate 8*)

AGE: TEENS AND ADULTS
TIME: MINUTES

The ultimate in decorated eggs is the folk-art technique of the Ukrainians, who create the most intricate patterns with a batik-like procedure of alternating waxing and progressively darker dyebaths.

A superb imitation can be done by anyone who has a steady hand and a bit of patience.

The egg photographed on page 72 was done with felt-tip pens. The thin black line surrounding each color area and the tiny geometric patterns give it the distinctively Ukrainian look.

NECESSITIES:
- One blown eggshell, primed
- Fiber-tipped pens with fine points
- Pencil (optional)
- Clear plastic spray or acrylic varnish

STEP-BY-STEP:

1. Divide the egg into working segments by making vertical and horizontal encircling lines with a yellow pen.

2. Starting at a center intersection, draw a series of geometric lines and shapes in different colors. Outline each color with black.

3. If pens with washable ink are used, the final coat must be a clear plastic spray. If permanent, waterproof markers are used, the final coat must be acrylic varnish.

EGGSHELL MOSAIC PLATE

(*Color Plate 3*)

AGE: TEENS AND ADULTS
TIME: HOURS

NECESSITIES:
- A plate (the illustrated one is 6″ in diameter)
- Blown eggshells (each one will cover approximately 10 square inches of surface; three were needed for the illustrated plate)
- Acrylic paint, black or other dark color
- Metallic gold model airplane paint
- Soft-haired brush, ½″ wide
- Toothpicks (optional)
- White glue
- Water jar for resting brush in, and for thinning glue
- Plate or other item to inlay
- Acrylic gel or matte varnish

STEP-BY-STEP:

1. Paint plate with black acrylic paint.
2. When dry, paint gold border.
3. Paint three eggshells (or an equivalent number of broken shells) gold. Allow 2–3 hours to dry sufficiently, to permit the kind of handling that will be necessary.

4. Break dry eggshells into pieces no larger than ½″ in any dimension.

5. Pour blob of glue onto a square of foil or other disposable surface. With brush, apply a small amount of glue near the edge of the plate. Press one piece of eggshell onto the glue. With tip of brush handle, tap on eggshell to crack it, then separate pieces of eggshell to let a bit of background paint show through between them. With practice, one can develop an angled jab that will crack and separate the piece of shell in one motion. (Some people find it easier to use their fingernail rather than the brush handle to crack the shell.)

6. Keep working around the edge of the plate and then towards the center. A nice effect is

achieved by varying the size of the shell pieces, from large at the edge to small towards the center, or vice versa.

7. When the plate is completely inlaid, secure the mosaics by brushing over them with a diluted mixture of glue and water. Let dry until the glue is no longer milky, but completely transparent. Then finish with a coat of acrylic gel (for a thick shiny finish) or acrylic matte varnish (for a satin finish).

ON YOUR OWN

• This same technique can be used to cover picture or mirror frames, little boxes, candlesticks, or other small items.

• Other colors can be used for the background, although dark colors look best.

• Other colors can be used for the mosaic pieces. They can be multicolored and placed at random, or colors can be placed in such a way as to build up a design or picture.

If you want to go on to advanced techniques in decorating eggs, there are two excellent books by Arden J. Newsome on the subject:

Egg Craft (New York: Lothrop, Lee & Shepard, 1973)

Egg Decorating Plain and Fancy (New York: Crown, 1973)

Food Additives and Discards

What do these things have in common: salt, spices, food coloring, chicken bones, and carrot tops? They can all be reincarnated as paint, kitchen accessories, jewelry, or note paper. Cupboard staples and food discards find their way into intriguing little projects.

FOOD COLOR FINGER PAINTINGS
(Color Plate 12)

AGE: ALL AGES
TIME: MINUTES

Here's a bit of now-you-see-it, now-you-don't magic that will amuse everyone from pre-schoolers to adults.

NECESSITIES:
- A piece of wax paper about 9″ × 12″ (plastic wrap will not do)
- Liquid food coloring
- Large white paper, such as shelf paper, for a working background

Optional:
- Iron and ironing surface
- Picture frame
- Construction paper and scissors

STEP-BY-STEP:

1. Fold the wax paper crosswise to 6″ × 9″ and sharpen the crease with the back of a fingernail.

2. Open the paper, and fairly near (but *not on*) the crease, squirt one drop of each of two or three food colors. Fold the paper closed again, and push the colored spots gently with the fingertips to move the colors around and make them blend. The white background paper makes the colors luminous and easy to see.

3. Unfold the paper, and—surprise!—there's *no* Rorschach blot; in fact there's nothing at all! The color has vanished. Fold the paper again, and the colors will reappear. (If there's no scientist in the family to explain the phenomenon, it's caused by the fact that wax paper normally repels the liquid. When the paper is folded and the air excluded, the color can be spread thinly between the surfaces. But as soon as the paper is opened, the liquid color beads up into nearly invisible specks.)

4. To preserve a pattern, simply press it with a warm iron. The heat will laminate the two layers of wax paper together, thus fixing the color.

5. Display the food color painting in either of these ways:
- Frame it against a white background.
- Put a border of construction paper around it and hang it in a window like stained glass.

FOOD COLOR MARBLEIZED PAPERS

(Color Plate 12)

AGE: ELEMENTARY SCHOOL AND UP
TIME: MINUTES

Drops of food coloring take on a life of their own in this automatic painting project.

NECESSITIES:
- Smooth paper, but not coated stock: some choices are typing paper, duplicating paper, notebook paper, filing cards. Young children can use a paper plate with a high rim to keep the paints from running over the edge
- Brush and water
- Liquid food coloring

STEP-BY-STEP:

1. Brush water over the paper, except for a one-inch margin all around. The paper should be damp, but not puddled.

2. Squeeze one drop of each desired food color on a different part of the moistened paper.

3. Lift the paper by the edges and tilt it at different angles to make the colors blend and swirl around.

4. Stop as soon as the color pattern is pleasing, and let the paper dry. Too much paper movement will make all the colors muddy.

• To make note paper, follow steps 8 through 11 under Hot-Tray Paintings, pages 134–135. The "On Your Own" suggestions there are also appropriate for marbleized papers. Food coloring marbleized note paper is pictured on Color Plate 12.

DIP-DYED PAPERS

(Color Plate 12)

AGE: ELEMENTARY SCHOOL AND UP
TIME: MINUTES

Beautiful circular or linear patterns can be made by dipping folded papers into food coloring. The paper traditionally used is Japanese rice paper, but it is rather expensive and usually available only at art shops. There are two very satisfactory substitutes.

NECESSITIES:
- White or pastel-colored tissue paper (for practicing and experiments)
    or
- Heavyweight or medium-weight silk span paper (for projects). This paper is sold at hobby shops for building model airplanes
- Liquid food coloring
- Paper towels
- Sectioned tray, such as muffin tin or TV-dinner tray
- Iron and ironing surface

STEP-BY-STEP:

1. Prepare the paper. Tissue or silk span paper must be slightly dampened to make it receptive to the dye. Cut either paper to the necessary size, and place it between two sheets of paper toweling which have been thoroughly wetted and thoroughly wrung out.

2. Prepare the dye. Squeeze about 10–20 drops of each food color into separate compartments. The color must be used full strength; the moisture in the paper will dilute it somewhat.

---

3. Fold the paper. There are two principal ways to fold the paper:
· Spoke-like through the center to produce circular designs

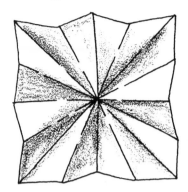

· Accordion folds to produce linear designs

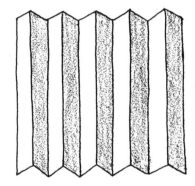

In both cases, fold back and forth; not in half and then in half again. The first method exposes all edges to the dye equally; the second conceals some edges inside and results in uneven dyeing.

4. Dip the paper. Hold and bend the basic folded paper in such a way that one corner or part of one side can be touched to the food coloring. Dip lightly and remove it quickly. Watch how far the color spreads; if necessary, help direct the color where desired by pressing the dyed area with the fingers. This pressing also assures that the dye will penetrate through all layers of the paper.

5. If the color does not cover as large an area as desired, dip it again.

6. Keep bending and dipping different parts of the paper until the pattern and colors are pleasing. With care, it is possible to open the paper to look at it, and then refold it if necessary to redip it.

7. When finished, unfold the paper and let it dry on several thicknesses of newspaper. To remove the folds, press the paper with a warm iron. The dry paper will not run, but guard against getting it wet.

This is one method of producing a circular pattern.

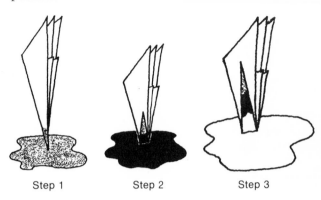

This is one method of producing a linear pattern.

ON YOUR OWN
· Frame and hang dip-dyed papers, or use them to cover books (page 79), boxes (page 78), or cans.

OCEAN-IN-A-BOTTLE

AGE: TEENS AND ADULTS
TIME: MINUTES

Have you ever seen a miniature ocean, a kinetic device which gives the effect of churning ocean waves? It sells for an exorbitant price in elegant shops. The secret is two incompatible liquids, which swirl around but never mix.

NECESSITIES:
- Water
- Liquid food coloring
- Turpentine
- A long narrow jar or other glass container which can be tightly capped. (An excellent small choice is the corked tube in which a vanilla bean is packed.)

STEP-BY-STEP:

1. Fill the container slightly less than half way with water. Add a drop each of blue and green food coloring (or whatever amount is required by the capacity of the container).

2. Fill the container to the top with turpentine. Seal tightly, trying to keep air bubbles out.

3. Hold the container sideways and tilt it up and down to see the effect of the rolling ocean.

4. Suspend it horizontally where it will sway with a breeze or the touch of a finger.

THREE NOVELTY PAINTS

STARCH PAINT

AGE: PRESCHOOL AND OLDER (TO USE)
        ADULT (TO PREPARE)
TIME: MINUTES

Starch paint was at one time the traditional way of decorating papers for bookbinding. Starch paper can also be used to cover boxes (page 78).

MIX IN SAUCEPAN:
- 2 TABLESPOONS CORNSTARCH
- 2 TABLESPOONS COLD WATER

ADD:
- 1 CUP BOILING WATER, STIRRING CONSTANTLY UNTIL MIXTURE COMES TO A BOIL AGAIN AND THICKENS.

Let cool. Then add enough acrylic paint to make the desired color (the amount varies with the hue selected and the deepness preferred).

NECESSITIES:
- Starch paint
- Paper
- Brush
- Texturing implements, such as a comb, fork, cardboard cut with zigzag edge, fingernails.

STEP-BY-STEP:

1. Brush starch paint onto paper.

2. Make designs by scraping one or more of the texturing implements across the paint.

FINGER PAINT

AGE: PRESCHOOL TO EARLY ELEMEN-
      TARY (TO USE)
      ADULT (TO PREPARE)
TIME: MINUTES

Finger paint is traditionally the first paint given to children because it is such a direct medium; there is no tool to come between the hands and the paint, and preschoolers relish the acceptability of this form of smearing. Besides, as parents all too often discover, even when children have paint brushes, they often end up finger-painting anyway!

- ½ CUP CORNSTARCH, DISSOLVED IN ¾ CUP COLD WATER IN 2-QUART SAUCEPAN
- 1 ENVELOPE UNFLAVORED GELATIN, SPRINKLED ON ¼ CUP COLD WATER
- 2 CUPS HOT WATER
- ½ CUP SOAP FLAKES OR DETERGENT POWDER
- THREE OR MORE 8-OZ. JARS WITH COVERS (JUNIOR BABY FOOD JARS ARE IDEAL)
- POWDERED OR LIQUID TEMPERA, RED, YELLOW, AND BLUE (GREEN, OPTIONAL)

Add hot water to cornstarch mixture and cook over medium heat, stirring constantly, until mixture comes to a boil and is clear and smooth.

Remove from heat, stir in softened gelatin, then soap, and stir until both are dissolved and the mixture is thick and smooth.

Divide finger paints among jars; leave an inch empty at the top. Add to each jar 1 tablespoon powdered tempera or 2 tablespoons liquid tempera. Stir until thoroughly mixed. Keep covered and refrigerated when not being used.

NECESSITIES:

- Finger paints
- Finger painting paper or glazed (not plastic) shelf paper, ideally 18″ × 24″
- Tongue depressors (optional)
- Working surface protected with plastic covering
- Sink (or bowl of water and sponge)
- Smock for child to wear

STEP-BY-STEP:

1. Wet both sides of paper under running water in sink, or with sponge. Press paper onto work surface and smooth out all air bubbles.

2. Put a dab of paint (with tongue depressor or finger) onto the paper. Spread it with hands. Use fingertips, knuckles, fingernails, and other parts of the hands and arms to make patterns on the paper.

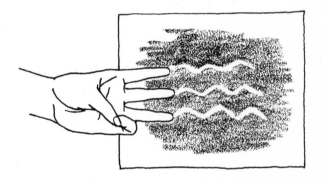

3. One color of paint is enough for beginners. Add colors when requested. Either red or blue is a good first color because they are so bright; yellow is a good second color because when mixed with the first, it will yield a recognizable secondary color (red and yellow make orange; blue and yellow make green).

SALT PAINT

AGE: PRE-TEEN
TIME: MINUTES

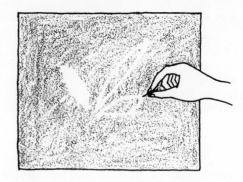

> MIX:
> · 2 PARTS SALT
> · 1 PART FLOUR
> GRADUALLY ADD:
>   ENOUGH WATER TO MAKE A SMOOTH PASTE

NECESSITIES:
· Salt paint
· Cardboard, paper plate, or other stiff paper
· Toothpick
· Spoon (optional)
· Paint (optional)

STEP-BY-STEP:
1. Dip toothpick into salt paint mixture and make an outline drawing on paper.

2. Use a spoon to fill mixture into the outline, if desired.

3. When dry, the pictures may be painted.

ON YOUR OWN
• On a black background, salt paint makes impressive-looking hieroglyphics.
• Try the technique for Halloween pictures, snow scenes, or fireworks.

LAYERED SPICES

AGE: TEENS AND ADULTS
TIME: MINUTES

This is a kitchen version of sand art, using the ground spices that come in harmonious shades of gold, red, and brown.

NECESSITIES:
· Small clear glass container such as a bud vase, test tube, prescription pill bottles
· Three or more of the following spices:
  Gold—curry powder, mustard powder, turmeric
  Red—paprika, cayenne, chili powder
  Brown—nutmeg, allspice, mace, cloves
  (Note: Do not use cinnamon; it is powdery and blurs the other spices.)
· Salt—to intersperse for contrast

STEP-BY-STEP:
1. Pour contrasting layers of spice into the container. Design interest is achieved by one of the following methods:
  · Vary the thickness of succeeding layers.
  · Tilt the container after pouring each layer so the layers themselves are of variable thickness.
  · For an icicle effect, slide a toothpick or needle between the glass and the spice. This can be done after each layer, or only at the end.
2. To prevent the spices from shifting, either insert a cork into the neck of the container and cap top tightly, or drip candle wax over the surface.

HERB NOTEPAPER

(*Color Plate 12*)

AGE: PRE-TEEN AND UP
TIME: MINUTES (WITH A SEVERAL WEEK
INTERVAL FOR DRYING HERBS)

Give ordinary note paper a unique personal touch.

NECESSITIES:
· Sprigs of fine-leaved herbs or vegetable tops, such as parsley, dill, carrot tops, etc.
· Facial or toilet tissue
· Heavy book, such as mail-order catalog or metropolitan area telephone book
· Blank notepaper from the stationery store
· Diluted white glue and brush

STEP-BY-STEP:
1. Spread each leaf sprig into an attractive form with a minimum of overlapping. Place each between a fold of tissue and insert it between the pages of a heavy book. Put additional books or heavy weights on it, and leave for two weeks while the leaves dry.

2. Brush diluted white glue onto backs of leaves, and affix to notepaper.

ON YOUR OWN
• The same technique can be used with thin, flat-leaved flowers, particularly pansies, and delicate-leaved weeds.
• With larger paper, this technique can be used for greeting cards. Some of the greens look like Christmas trees; others can be arranged to resemble wreaths. Add painted ribbons or berries. To make it look more like a greeting card and to give the added protection necessary for display, cover the front with transparent, self-sticking, vinyl contact paper.

WISHBONE NECKLACE

(*Color Plate 5*)

AGE: TEENS AND ADULTS
TIME: HOURS, SPREAD OVER A DAY OR
TWO

If you can persuade your family to stop making wishes long enough to accumulate some wishbones, a strikingly beautiful necklace can be made.

NECESSITIES:
· Chicken wishbones (7 will cover the front of the neck, from shoulder to shoulder; 11 will completely encircle the neck)
· Steel wool or plastic scrubber
· Drill with $\frac{1}{16}''$ bit
· Silver metallic model airplane paint
· Metallic silver sewing thread
· Crochet hook, size 2 (optional)
· Necklace clasps
· White glue

STEP-BY-STEP:
1. As the wishbones accumulate, scrub each one clean and let it dry.
2. Drill a $\frac{1}{16}''$ diameter hole at both forked ends of each wishbone.

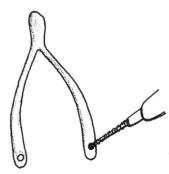

3. Paint the wishbones silver.

4. With crochet hook or with fingers, make a chain from the metallic silver thread the length that the necklace is to be.

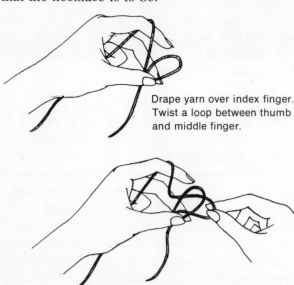

Drape yarn over index finger. Twist a loop between thumb and middle finger.

Bring straight yarn into loop. Pull to tighten for a new loop. Continue. End chain by pulling the cut end of yarn through the final loop.

5. Thread the wishbones onto the chain. Tie the chain ends to necklace clasps. Secure with a dot of white glue; when dry, cut off thread ends.

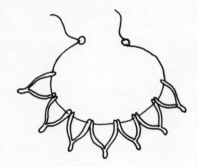

ON YOUR OWN

• A wishbone necklace could also be drilled and threaded at the opposite end.

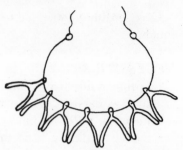

• Try making necklaces from other bones. For a more primitive look, simply varnish the bones instead of painting them.
• A budding archaeologist or future doctor might enjoy reconstructing a real or fanciful animal from an assortment of bones.
• Bones, alone or combined with pebbles, can make an interesting textural relief.
• Beef marrow bones, cut in $1''$ or $1\frac{1}{2}''$ lengths, make unusual napkin rings.

Equipment and Supplies

Here is a smorgasbord of ideas for using the electric mixer, hot tray, paper plates, packaging materials, wax paper, and—to wrap it all up—aluminum foil.

RAFFIA

An electric mixer provides a short-cut for making raffia from crepe paper. It twists the paper tighter and faster than can be done by hand.

NECESSITIES:
- Electric mixer, preferably a portable model
- Crepe paper
- A second person, to help

STEP-BY-STEP:

1. Cut crepe paper into strips either 1″ or 2″ wide. Wider strips will yield thicker raffia.

2. Tie one end of the crepe paper to the bottom of the beater.

3. One person should operate the beater, while the second one holds the other end of the crepe paper across the room.

AGE: ELEMENTARY SCHOOL (WITH ASSISTANCE) AND UP
TIME: MINUTES

4. Turn the motor to the lowest speed and hold the beater horizontally. As it turns, the paper will gradually twist. Stop when it is at the desired tightness.

5. When the paper is reaching the limit of its twistability, both people will feel it pull tighter. The motor *must* be turned off at that point, or the paper will tear.

6. If the paper has been twisted as tightly as possible, it can be made to twine itself into a rope. One person holds the center point tightly while the other person holds the two ends together. Let go of the center, and the two halves will snap together into a tightly twined rope that will not come apart.

7. Use the raffia for wrapping (see page 159 and follow directions for yarn wrapping).

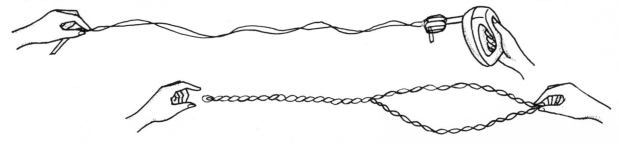

HOT TRAY PAINTINGS

(*Color Plate 12*)

This is one of those marvelous activities that children can do every bit as well as adults, and that every age will find fascinating. It is up to each parent, however, to decide whether his or her child should work with hot equipment.

NECESSITIES:
- Electric hot tray
- Heavy-duty aluminum foil
- Crayons
- Paper towels
- Various kinds of paper: typing, tissue, rice paper, silk span paper, posterboard, etc.
- Colored construction paper
- Two L-shaped pieces of stiff paper or cardboard
- Pencil, ruler, scissors, rubber cement

STEP-BY-STEP:

1. Cover the entire surface of the hot tray, including the handles and the sides, with aluminum foil as a protection against melted crayon wax. Lay another smaller piece of foil over the heated part only. Turn the heat on to medium.

2. Draw or make designs on the foil with crayons, which will melt as soon as they touch

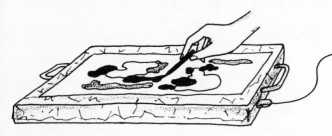

the hot foil. When the pattern looks pleasing, lay a piece of paper on it, press it with a folded wad of paper towel to get an imprint, then lift off the paper. Set it aside and continue drawing and making prints.

3. Some crayon will remain on the foil; it may either be left there while adding more crayons for the next print, or it may be wiped away with paper towels before the next design is started.

4. Use as many different kinds of paper as possible to see the different effects on each.

5. Try different kinds of crayons, too. Pressed crayons (which are larger and less waxy than standard crayons) melt more slowly and give a more textured surface. Fluorescent crayons are bright and delicate. Metallic crayons shimmer.

6. Lift off the paper in different ways: straight up, sliding in one direction, or rotating it slightly.

7. When finished, disconnect the hot tray and set it aside to cool.

8. The true beauty of the designs will show up after they are trimmed and framed. Move the two L-shaped papers on the painting until the most attractive part has been isolated. Mark the outline with pencil, and cut it out. Do the same with all the paintings.

9. For each little painting, select a color of construction paper which most enchances it. Lay

---

the painting on the construction paper and mark a small margin around it. Cut the construction paper twice as large as marked.

10. Fold the construction paper in half, attach the painting on the front with rubber cement, press, and let dry.

11. Use these notes for informal correspondence or for greeting cards.

ON YOUR OWN
• Melted crayon paintings can be used like other decorative papers except they should not be sharply folded because the wax will crack. However, they may be wrapped around cans.
• Cut a construction paper frame and put the painting behind it.
• A group of melted crayon paintings, done in similar colors, can be mounted on a colored background (or matted) and framed.
• There are three other ways that melted crayon paintings can be made into note paper:
  · Paste them onto blank notepaper instead of construction paper.
  · Use the front of blank notepaper itself to press onto the melted crayon design.
  · Make a French-fold card with an opening on the front to frame the crayon painting.

Cut paper twice as long and twice as wide as the crayon painting. Fold paper in half downward, then in half from left to right.

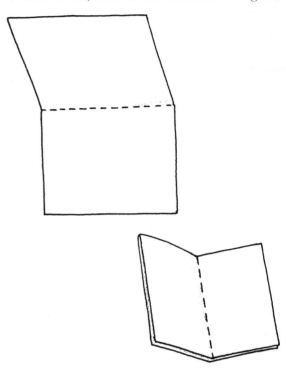

Cut out window in first layer of paper and slip crayon painting behind the opening, securing it with rubber cement at the corners.

• For a related project with melted crayons, see Wax Paper Transparencies, page 145.

PAPER PLATE FOOD COLLAGE

AGE: PRESCHOOL
TIME: MINUTES

A child who is able to cut and paste can be motivated to learn about food through this activity. Unobtrusive teaching results in the best learning.

NECESSITIES:
- Paper plates
- Photographs of food from magazines and/or can labels and frozen food wrappers
- Scissors
- White paste (see Thick Paste, page 41)

STEP-BY-STEP:
1. Cut out pictures of foods.
2. Paste several on each paper plate to look like a meal serving.

ON YOUR OWN
- Make one breakfast plate, one lunch plate, and one dinner plate. The child's food selections offer a good take-off point for simple discussions of nutrition: Do the three plates contain a child's nutritional needs for one day? Do the foods go well together in terms of taste, appearance?
- A more imaginative version of this project, for older children, is to design one's own foods with colored construction paper. Dinner, for instance, could be a round brown circle (hamburger), little green circles (peas), small red squares (diced beets), long orange triangles (carrots). Maybe a yellow crescent (banana) or a red circle (apple) for dessert. Note the opportunities for teaching about colors and shapes.
- Save those mouth-watering photographs that accompany magazine recipes. When there are enough, cover a kitchen wall with a collage, or use them to refinish kitchen cabinets instead of repainting. In either case, protect collaged papers with varnish.

PAPER PLATE ORNAMENTS

STAR CIRCLES

AGE: ELEMENTARY SCHOOL AND UP
TIME: MINUTES

NECESSITIES:
- Paper plates, white and/or colored
- Scissors
- Construction paper, various colors
- White glue
- Thread for hanging

STEP-BY-STEP:
1. Cut away the rim of the paper plates; keep only the flat center.
2. Cut colored construction paper into 12 circles half the diameter of the paper plate circle.

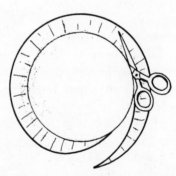

Fold the small circles in half, and cut slits from the fold halfway to the outer rim.

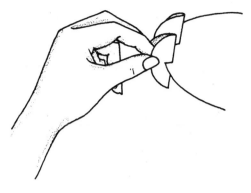

3. Slide the small circles onto the edge of the paper plate circle, and let them unfold slightly so that they touch each other. Squeeze a dot of glue at each "V" fold.

4. Attach a thread either at the center of the circle so the ornament hangs horizontally, or on the outer edge so it hangs vertically.

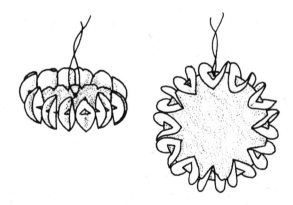

ON YOUR OWN

• Vary the number and size of the circles around the edge.

SPIRALS

AGE: ELEMENTARY SCHOOL
TIME: MINUTES

NECESSITIES:
  · Paper plates, preferably different color front and back
  · Scissors
  · Thread or yarn for hanging

STEP-BY-STEP:

1. Cut paper plate in a spiral from the edge to the center.

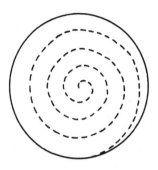

2. Attach a thread at the center by which to hang the ornament. Twirl it, first in one direction and then in the other, for the optical illusion of ascending and descending motion.

SPONGE COLLAGE

Kitchen sponges (unused ones, please!) can be cut and glued to a styrofoam tray or other background.

NECESSITIES:
- Kitchen sponges in assorted colors
- Scissors
- Styrofoam tray or cardboard
- White glue

STEP-BY-STEP:

1. Cut sponges into desired shapes, and arrange them on backing.

2. When the arrangement is satisfactory, glue each piece of sponge to the background.

ON YOUR OWN
- Cut thin slices of pink sponge into little oblongs and paste them onto milk carton buildings (next project) to represent bricks.
- Cut a sponge into a fish shape for a baby's bath toy.
- Cut sponges of varied colors into thin squares to use for mosaic pictures.

MILK CARTON VILLAGE
(*Color Plate 10*)

The buildings that make up cities, towns, villages, and farms are important play accessories for children. Read the section "Play Town" on page 80 for basic general information before starting this project. That project is a wrapping and printing method of making buildings; this one is a paint and collage method.

NECESSITIES:
- Milk and cream cartons, rinsed and dried
- Acrylic gesso and paint
- Tempera paint (optional)
- Magazine pictures of roof tiles, windows, doors, bricks, grass, and trees
- Magazine pictures of interiors: appliances, furniture (optional)
- Other papers and collage materials that look like house parts (optional)
- White glue

STEP-BY-STEP:

1. Shape and assemble the cartons into the kinds of buildings required.

2. Prime them with a coat of gesso to help conceal the printing and make the paint adhere better. Then paint them the desired color. If tempera paint is used, preschoolers can participate in this step.

3. Decorate the buildings in one or more of the following ways:

· Select appropriate pictures and paste windows, doors, etc., where they are wanted. If there aren't as many pictures as necessary, add them later to make this a continuing project, or use alternative decorations. (The reason for interior scenes is that children sometimes go through a stage of wanting to include what they *know* is inside, even if it is concealed by walls; they would want to paste pictures showing the bedroom, kitchen, living room, etc.)

· Cut shapes from self-sticking vinyl contact paper to represent building features. Brick and wood-grain patterns are available. Sections of berry baskets can look like windows.

· Paint decorative features.

4. If tempera paint is used, an adult should seal the finished buildings with a coat of varnish.

ON YOUR OWN

• Play sets which are replicas of fast food chains or motels can be made by pasting emblems from the company's ads onto buildings fashioned from milk cartons or from supermarket cartons.

MILK CARTON WRAP-AROUNDS

(*Color Plate 10*)

There's no need to settle for anonymous trucks and cars when children can design the specific vehicles they want for their play: an ice cream truck, school bus, camper, fire engine, moving van, or whatever.

NECESSITIES:
· Half-gallon milk cartons, rinsed and dried
· Scissors
· Tape
· Supermarket bags or kraft paper
· Pencil
· Tempera paints
· White glue
· Shellac (to be used by adult)

STEP-BY-STEP:
1. Make a pattern by removing the peaked top of one milk carton, and cutting and flattening the rest of it, as illustrated. Tape the bottom from a second milk carton, opposite the bottom extension. The pattern can be re-used indefinitely.

2. Trace around the pattern on paper, adding

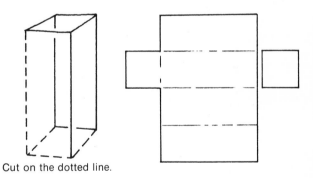

Cut on the dotted line.

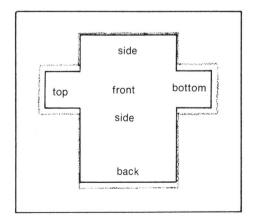

side

top   front   bottom

side

back

---

seam allowance where shown. Paint the parts which will become the top, front, back, and sides of the vehicle.

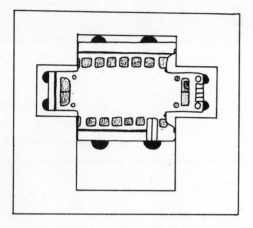

3. Flatten the peaked top of the carton to be wrapped, as shown on page 81.

4. Cut out the paper wrapping and glue it around the carton, starting with the seam allowances.

5. An adult should shellac the finished vehicle.

ON YOUR OWN
• Most children under the age of six or seven (and some older ones) have difficulty visualizing the relationship of the parts of the vehicle on a flat paper. They may prefer to wrap the carton first and paint it afterwards. Or, the vehicle may be painted on a gessoed, rather than a wrapped, carton.

• Patterns can be made similarly for other size milk cartons.

MILK CARTON TRAIN

NECESSITIES:
· Half-gallon milk cartons, rinsed and dried
· Scissors (for children) or craft knife (for adults)
· Tempera paints
· Shellac (for use by adult)
· String or cord
· Toothpicks or wooden matchsticks

STEP-BY-STEP:
1. Make milk cartons into train cars.
· For locomotive, tape closed the peaked top of one carton.
· Flatten tops of all other cartons as shown on page 81.
· For freight cars, cut away one side of each carton; the open side will be the top.
· For passenger cars, if openings are wanted for windows, cut them now; otherwise, set the cartons aside and paint the windows later.

AGE: ELEMENTARY SCHOOL AND UP (TO MAKE)
PRESCHOOL AND ELEMENTARY
SCHOOL (TO USE)
TIME: MINUTES TO HOURS, PLUS INTER-
VALS FOR DRYING

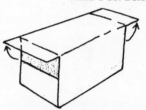

· For caboose, lay carton on side and cut a flap as shown on the front and back. Turn flaps up to form roof extensions. If necessary, support the extensions by taping cardboard or a popsicle stick underneath.
· A round salt or cereal box can be combined with a lengthwise half of a milk carton to become an old-style locomotive or a tank car.

2. Paint the locomotive black, the caboose red, and the other cars as desired. If the tempera is not ahdering well, either mix a few drops of liquid detergent into it, or precoat all the cartons with gesso.

3. An adult should seal all the cars with shellac.

4. Punch a hole in the center of the front and back of each car to be joined to another. For open cars, push cord through the hole and tie a knot on the inside. For closed cars, tape end of cord onto a 1″ length of toothpick or wooden matchstick. Insert through hole and pull so that the wood is lodged crosswise against the hole. There should be about one inch of cord between cars.

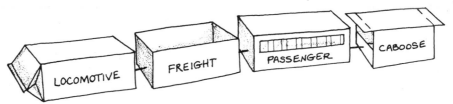

CRAYON RESIST CONTAINER
(*Color Plate 6*)

AGE: PRESCHOOL (WITH HELP) AND UP
TIME: MINUTES, PLUS INTERVALS FOR DRYING

The technique of crayon resist is a simplified version of batik. Children find it very exciting the first time they see it. It is based on the fact that the waxy crayon will repel the water-based paint applied afterward, and will show through. The effect is most dramatic with light-colored crayons and black paint.

NECESSITIES:
- A one-gallon milk carton
- White posterboard
- White glue
- Light and bright-colored crayons
- Black tempera paint and brush
- Shellac (to be applied by adult)

STEP-BY-STEP:

1. Cut away the peaked top of the milk carton; wash and dry the inside.

2. Wrap and glue posterboard around the sides of the carton. Press sharp creases at corners.

3. With crayons, scribble, write a name, or make a drawing or design on the posterboard. The larger the crayoned area, the more attractive the finished container will be.

4. Paint the entire container, inside and out, with black tempera.

5. When dry, an adult should shellac the entire surface.

ON YOUR OWN
- Use the container to store children's crayons or small toys, or for a small paper basket.
- The posterboard can also be wrapped around cans or other round containers.
- Use the same technique on smaller milk or cream cartons, which would be suitable for holding pencils or other small items. Small cartons do not require the extra support of a posterboard wrapping. Instead, they may simply be coated with gesso, then crayoned and painted.
- The crayon resist technique can also be used for drawings. Brush black tempera over an orange jack-o'-lantern for a Halloween picture, over white dots for a snow scene, or over a daytime drawing with the sun to change it to a nighttime drawing with the moon.

CARDBOARD TUBE NAPKIN RINGS

AGE: TEENS AND ADULTS
TIME: MINUTES, WITH INTERVALS FOR
DRYING

(*Color Plate 7*)

All your ingenuity and originality can go into these delightful little items. They are lovely to use at home or to give as gifts.

NECESSITIES:
- Cardboard tubes
- Ruler and craft knife
- Acrylic gesso
- Paints, decorative papers, yarn, and other trimmings
- Acrylic medium or varnish

STEP-BY-STEP:
1. Cut cardboard tubes into 1½″ lengths.
2. Seal inside and outside with one coat of gesso (if another color paint will be superimposed) or two coats (if the white background is to show).
3. Decorate as desired. Here are some suggestions:
   - Wrap with raffia or yarn.
   - Attach self-sticking tapes or other shapes.
   - Wrap with dip-dyed paper (see Dip-dyed Paper, page 126).
   - Wrap with potato-printed paper (see Gift Box, page 78).
   - Collage it to look like tortoiseshell (see Mock Tortoiseshell Snack Tray, page 144).
   - Most suggestions for decorating eggs (pages 111–124) are appropriate.
4. Finish with the appropriate sealer, as recommended in the project consulted.

EGG CARTON ORNAMENTS

AGE: PRE-TEENS AND UP
TIME: HOURS, SPREAD OVER A DAY OR
MORE

(*Color Plate 9*)

Pressed cardboard egg cartons can be cut and folded, twisted, or glued into rearranged shapes that belie their mundane origin. They can be further enhanced by imaginative painting. Have plenty of cartons on hand because a lot of inspirations come during the cutting and glueing process.

NECESSITIES:
- Pressed cardboard egg cartons
- Scissors
- White glue
- Acrylic gesso
- Paints, preferably fluorescent tempera or metallic airplane paints. Plain tempera or acrylic paints may also be used.
- Yarn for hanging

STEP-BY-STEP:
1. Cut egg cartons into segments and glue them into desired configurations. The following diagram shows some techniques for the base of two carton sections by six carton sections. (Similar, but not identical, arrangements can be made from three carton sections by four carton sections.)

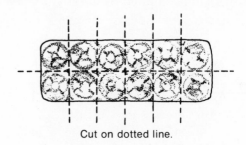

Cut on dotted line.

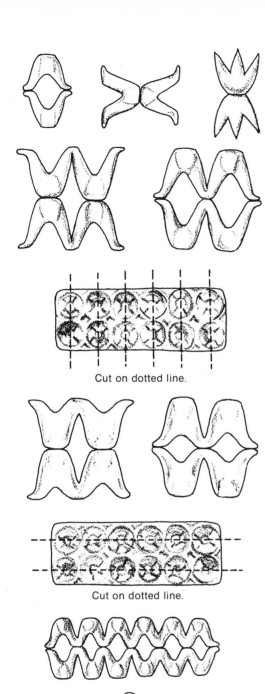

Cut on dotted line.

Cut on dotted line.

2. When glue is dry, seal with acrylic gesso.

3. Paint as desired. Some ideas to try are:

· Use different colors for the inside and outside surfaces. (It's easier to paint the inside first.)

· Change colors in unexpected places: where two planes meet, for instance, rather than where two pieces meet.

· Use a contrasting color along the edges.

4. Insert a loop of matching or contrasting yarn through the finished ornament for hanging.

ON YOUR OWN

• Hang a group of identical or related ornaments around a horizontally-suspended embroidery hoop.

• Assemble large flat ornaments in multiples to cover a wall.

• Styrofoam egg cartons make good disposable paint-mixing cups.

• Use the individual compartments to teach children sorting, counting, multiplying, and dividing.

• Cut styrofoam egg cartons into parts to assemble into miniature furniture.

MOCK TORTOISESHELL SNACK TRAYS

(*Color Plate 7*)

AGE: ADULT
TIME: MINUTES, SPREAD OUT
OVER SEVERAL DAYS

This is a tissue collage technique for making snack trays which are washable in hot soapy water.

NECESSITIES:
- Styrofoam trays (Use the $4\frac{1}{2}'' \times 8\frac{1}{2}''$ size for a set of individual trays, or a larger size for a serving tray.)
- Tissue paper, brown and orange
- Acrylic gloss medium and brush
- Polyester resin and glue brush
- Lacquer thinner, for cleaning glue brush

STEP-BY-STEP:

1. For each tray tear four pieces of tissue paper as follows:
   - One of each color slightly larger than the tray
   - One of each color slightly smaller than the tray

Torn edges look better than cut edges. Crumple the papers slightly. Save slivers of leftover brown.

2. Brush the top of the tray with acrylic medium. Place the larger piece of brown tissue on it, and brush with more medium. Let the paper wrinkle. Arrange a few slivers of brown tissue to simulate the darker tortoiseshell shadings. Place large orange tissue on top and brush with medium. Let the overhang remain dry, and set the tray aside to dry.

3. Repeat on bottom of tray, first folding back overhang, then applying smaller papers. Let dry.

4. The next day, start the polyester resin finish. The top and bottom of the tray must each be done in a separate step. Mix a small amount ($\frac{1}{2}$ ounce is sufficient for each tray bottom) according to instructions, brush it on the bottom, and let harden overnight. Clean brush immediately in lacquer thinner.

5. The following day, mix a larger amount of polyester resin (2 ounces per tray). Brush part of it on the rim and pour the remainder into the tray. Let it harden overnight. Clean brush immediately in lacquer thinner.

NOTE: Resin dissolves raw styrofoam and even eats through some paints. Before using resin on snack trays prepared with any other collage materials, be sure to test the resin on a sample. If the styrofoam dissolves, seal the trays instead with polyurethane varnish. Varnished trays can be wiped with a damp cloth, but will not withstand washing as well as those coated with resin.

PLASTIC CAN LID COASTERS

(*Color Plate 7*)

AGE: TEENS AND ADULTS (YOUNGER
PEOPLE MIGHT ENJOY MAKING
JUST THE DESIGN CUT-OUTS)
TIME: MINUTES, WITH INTERVALS FOR DRYING

NECESSITIES:
- Plastic can lids of various diameters
- Acrylic paints
- Colored papers, preferably circular origami paper
- Scissors
- Contact cement
- Rubber cement
- Transparent self-adhesive vinyl contact paper
- Polyurethane varnish

STEP-BY-STEP:

1. Paint the outside of the plastic lid and the entire rim to match one of the paper colors.

2. Cut a paper circle (or select an origami circle) that just fits inside the can lid. Fold and cut one or more additional pieces of paper into patterns to superimpose on the background color. (See page 53 for suggestions on cutting origami paper patterns.)

3. Attach all layers of paper with rubber cement.

4. Seal the design with transparent self-adhesive vinyl contact paper. The easiest way to get it on smoothly is to cut a piece slightly larger than the circle, remove the paper backing, place the vinyl sticky side up, fold the origami paper right side down, and gently press the paper onto the vinyl, letting the center touch first and then lowering the sides. Cut away the excess vinyl.

5. Attach the circle design to the inside of the plastic lid with contact cement.

6. Varnish the painted part of the plastic lid.

ON YOUR OWN

• Make coasters into hanging ornaments or giant pendants by attaching a cord through the rim. In this case, the papers do not have to be sealed. (Color Plate 3)

• Group a number of coasters on a plaque, or line them up on a velvet ribbon as a wall decoration.

• Plastic lids can also be decorated in the following ways:

· Tissue paper collage: Prime the lid with a coat of gesso, then follow directions for Tissue Collage Egg, page 118.

· Seeds and beans: See instructions for samplers on page 103.

· Draw designs with permanent felt-tip or fiber-tip markers. (Don't use the water-soluble markers; they will smudge.) To make changes or corrections with permanent markers, remove color by rubbing with alcohol. Hang the ornament in a window, and it will look like stained glass. The effect is improved by surrounding each color with a black outline.

WAX PAPER TRANSPARENCIES

AGE: PRE-TEEN AND UP (OR YOUNGER, WITH ADULT HELP WITH THE IRON)
TIME: MINUTES

The heat of an iron will bond two sheets of wax paper together. This simple fact is the basis of some interesting laminates.

NECESSITIES:
· Wax paper
· Crayons
· A grater
· Colored tissue papers cut or torn into small pieces
· Bits of colored cellophane, yarn, leaves, foil, sequins, etc. (optional)
· Iron, ironing board, and protective cover, such as old sheet or paper towels
· White posterboard or other heavy paper

STEP-BY-STEP:

1. Lay a sheet of wax paper on the protected ironing board.

2. Sprinkle or arrange on it any one or combination of the following: crayon gratings, colored papers, or other flat decorative items.

3. Lay a second sheet of wax paper on top and press with a warm iron. Don't slide the iron; just press and lift.

4. When the laminated paper has cooled, cut it to the desired size and mount it on a white backing. Or hang it in the window where light can filter through.

ON YOUR OWN

• Make wax paper laminates into place mats by covering both sides with transparent self-sticking vinyl contact paper, or by inserting them into clear vinyl envelopes which are specially designed for making one's own place mats.

• Frame them, individually or in a group, to hang on the wall.

• Cut them to fit into transparent plastic can lids, and hang them in the window.

• For another project with wax paper, see Food Color Finger Paintings, page 125.

FOIL-WRAPPED BOTTLE

(*Color Plate 6*)

AGE: TEENS AND ADULTS
TIME: MINUTES

Two common objects come together as an elegant room accessory, thereby proving that the whole is greater than the sum of its parts.

NECESSITIES:
· An empty bottle
· White glue
· Heavy-duty aluminum foil
· Black acrylic paint, medium, and brush
· Paper towels

STEP-BY-STEP:

1. Cut the foil two inches longer than the bottle and two inches wider than the circumference at its widest part.

2. Crumple the foil to wrinkle it uniformly all over. Squeeze lightly for a high relief surface, or hard for a fine-grained appearance. Then gently stretch the foil back to nearly its original size. Work slowly and carefully to avoid tearing the foil.

3. Brush glue over the bottle and wrap the foil around it, dull side out. If there is a great difference between the circumference of the neck and the rest of the bottle, cut away some of the excess foil at the top in order to eliminate bulk. Pinch raw edges together and turn them under.

4. Press the foil against the bottle to flatten the wrinkles and reveal the pattern. Use either the fingers alone or also a burnishing tool such as a

brush handle or the side of a jar. Inside the neck, press with a paint brush handle.

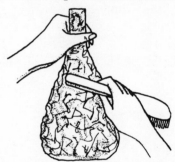

5. To antique the foil, brush it with black acrylic paint which has been diluted enough so it can flow into the crevices of the foil.

6. Let the paint set for a minute or two, then rub with paper towels to remove paint from the high parts. More rubbing will brighten and lighten the foil.

7. Use the bottle as a vase for fresh, dried, or artificial flowers or foliage.

ON YOUR OWN

• India ink can also be used for antiquing; it gives a slightly darker effect, somewhat like pewter.

• Experiment with the many textural variations that can be achieved by different degrees of pressing the foil both before and after covering the bottle.

• Make an "antique silver" picture frame from a plain wooden or plastic one. Lay the frame on a pre-crumpled piece of foil with enough margin to wrap around the back. Cut as illustrated. Wrap and finish, following instructions for the bottle.

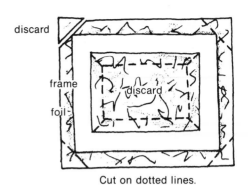

Cut on dotted lines.

ALUMINUM FOIL JEWELRY

AGE: TEENS AND ADULTS
TIME: MINUTES

Aluminum foil can be wrapped around a variety of bases to make brooches and pendants ranging in style from heirloom antique to art deco modern.

ANTIQUE BROOCH

NECESSITIES:
· Bases, such as jar lids or cardboard, about 2–3″ across
· White glue
· Heavy-duty aluminum foil
· Black acrylic paint, medium, and brush
· Paper towels
· Pin clasp
· Contact cement

STEP-BY-STEP:
1. Follow the same procedure for covering the bottle in the previous project.
2. Affix a pin clasp on back with contact cement. If desired, a chain may be looped through the pin clasp to make the brooch into a pendant.

MODERN BROOCH
(*Color Plates 4 and 5*)
The modern brooch features smooth foil and gets its textural interest from built-up layers on the base.

NECESSITIES:
· Cardboard
· Ruler, pencil, compass, scissors
· White glue and brush
· Permanent ink fiber-tip pens
· Pin clasp
· Contact cement

STEP-BY-STEP:
1. Cut cardboard into geometric shapes, between 2–3″ across.
2. Cut smaller segments of the base shape and glue them onto the base. For a circle, use wedges of decreasing angle or smaller concentric circles. For a square, try rectangles of gradually decreasing width or a series of smaller squares.

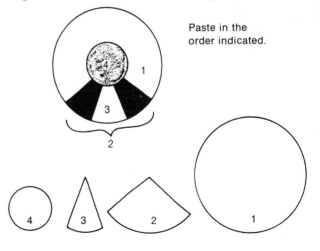

Paste in the order indicated.

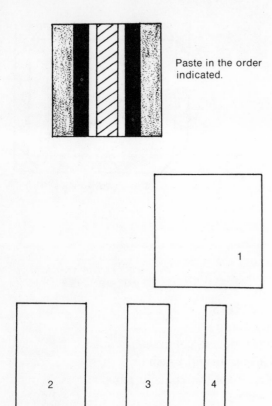

Paste in the order indicated.

3. Brush the surface of the built-up base with glue, and wrap a smooth piece of foil around it, dull side outward. Press the foil with the fingertips, beginning in the center and working outwards, so that the contour of the base is sharply reproduced on the foil.

4. Add metallic contrasts with permanent ink fiber-tip pens. For "gold" use light tan; for "copper," use brown.

5. Affix a pin clasp on back with contact cement. If desired, a chain can be looped through the pin clasp to make the brooch into a pendant.

ON YOUR OWN
• Other things besides cardboard layers can be used to create texture on the base. Try a design of round toothpicks, or a piece cut from a plastic berry box or tomato box. See Aluminum Foil Printmaking (page 85) for additional ideas.

• Larger pieces of textured cardboard that are covered with foil may be used as printing plates.

Multimedia: Drama and Music

There are *two* specific things to make, each representing a category of essential playthings for children: puppets and rhythm instruments.

The materials and methods of making them range from simple to complex; the object is not only that of making usable play materials, but also of accumulating a repertoire of techniques which can be adapted to other play materials and to more advanced crafts.

There are adults who have carried their play interests into adulthood, creating dollhouses, puppets, and other replicas of toys with painstaking details and intricate craftsmanship. These are objects to look at and admire, but not to play with.

But that is not the goal of this book. The items in this chapter are intended as play materials, so no really advanced techniques are included. In fact, if making any of these things for children who are still too young to do part or all of the job alone, it is best to stick to an ability level that can be understood by a child. A child should be encouraged to feel that he or she can also tackle these projects, rather than finding them so elaborate that a parent must be asked to do them. Don't let complicated techniques get in the way of spontaneous play.

Puppets * * * * * * * * * * * * * *

Beginning somewhere around the age of three, puppets become important playthings for children. A child's first puppet may well represent himself. Later, puppets play the following other roles in child's play:

• A puppet can be a companion, someone to talk with.

• A puppet can help a child pretend to be someone or something else — a prince or a princess, a grownup, an animal.

• A puppet can help a child cope with fears. If he has a witch or a monster puppet, then he can *control* the witch or monster and thereby subdue the fear. (This is why children often select spooky costumes for Halloween.)

• A puppet can help a shy child talk more easily; with attention focused on the puppet, the child can often let the puppet say things that he cannot otherwise bring himself to say. Also, he will often accept what a parent says through a puppet more readily than what the parent says directly. Parent-child communication can often be enhanced if they both have puppets.

• A puppet can help a child work off aggressions

in an acceptable way. If the puppet can say the bad words or engage in a Punch and Judy show, then the child himself may be relieved of the need to curse or fight.

A three-year-old's puppets merely talk; but a four-year-old's puppets begin to act. Little scenes that the child improvises will require a simple stage, which can easily be made by cutting an opening in a carton. By the age of five the child will probably want something a little more formal, with curtains or a screening arrangement to mark the beginning and end of the show.

In short, children use puppets in different ways at different ages. For the very youngest, puppets represent a way of self-expression. For older children, they offer an opportunity to act out real or imaginary situations.

Toward the later elementary school years, children like the formality of a written playscript, appropriately costumed puppets, a stage setting, and all the accoutrements of a proper dramatic experience. Since this is more than one person can do alone, the interest comes, appropriately enough, at just the age when children prefer to work in groups. Their performances are often superb. The stage is set for these productions in the spontaneous self-expressive play of the earliest years.

STICK PUPPETS

These are the very simplest kinds of puppets because there are no moving parts and they can be handled easily by even the youngest child.

WOODEN SPOON PUPPET
(*Color Plate 11*)

Paint or paste features onto the back of the bowl. (If it's a spoon that will be used again later, select self-sticking features that can easily be peeled off.)

POPSICLE STICK PUPPET

Paste the stick between two circles of paper. Draw features with felt-tip marker or crayon.

Or, if the child is at the stage of drawing "big head" people, cut out one of those and a matching-size piece of blank paper, and paste the Popsicle stick between them.

PAPER BAG PUPPETS

Paper bag puppets are a transition from the non-manipulated puppet to the one whose head and arms are manipulated by the movements of three fingers. They start simply and gradually introduce the child to specific finger movements.

FIRST-FACED PUPPET

This simple one can be used even before a child can do any finger manipulations. Simply paste, paint, or draw features on an upside-down paper bag, and slip it over the child's fist. Attach to wrist with a fairly loose cord or ribbon tied around the neck of the bag.

STUFFED-FACE PUPPET

Some children don't like their hands confined; they would prefer this puppet whose face is stuffed with torn newspapers. Push a stick the length of the bag nearly to the top; tie a string around the neck. Manipulate the puppet by the stick.

A slightly more advanced version of this eliminates the stick and lets the child put his hand into the bag and slip one finger through the tied neck. This introduces the child to finger manipulation of the head.

MOVING MOUTH PUPPET

A child who can move four fingers simultaneously to meet his thumb is ready for a mouth-moving paper bag puppet. Before even beginning to decorate it, show the child how the bottom of the bag works. Open and close the flap, and point out where the mouth will go. Then draw on the

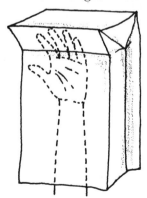

mouth, and give the child a chance to manipulate it. Once this has been tried, the parts all become

clearer. Draw or paint the rest of the face on the bag, or let the child do it if he or she wants to.

A previously-drawn face can be made into a moving mouth paper bag puppet. Cut the face through the middle of the mouth; paste the upper part on the bag flap, and the jaw part on the side of the bag.

MOVING EYES PUPPET

This time, it is the eyes that are put where the folded bottom meets the side, so that the eyes can open and close. If an open mouth is one of the facial features, it will look like a yawn when the eyes are closed, and like a gasp of surprise when the eyes are opened.

MOVING EARS PUPPET

A child's own fingers can become the ears of a rabbit or dog. Poke two holes in the top of the bag through which the child's fingers can wiggle.

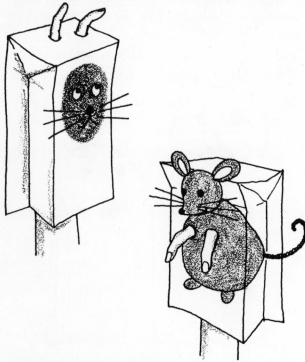

MOVING PAWS PUPPET

A child's fingers can become the paws of a gerbil, mouse, squirrel, or kangaroo. Poke two holes in the front of the bag through which the child's fingers can wiggle.

FINGER PUPPETS
(*Color Plate 11*)

The appeal of finger puppets is that a child can re-enact a story with many characters, with the whole cast right on hand, so to speak. No need to doff and don a different puppet for each line of dialogue. Finger puppets are just the thing for fairy tales. Simply move the appropriate finger forward to show who is speaking.

Some egg boxes have tall narrow cup dividers that are tapered just right to fit on either a child's or adult's fingers. (Finger puppets can also be made by wrapping construction paper around cake-decorating points, or by cutting the finger-tips from torn kitchen gloves.) Draw dainty faces with fiber-tip pens, and use tempera for larger features.

It is even possible to glue on appendages, as illustrated with the wolf in the Little Red Riding Hood cast. His mouth was formed from an extra egg divider, and the ears are points left over from cutting. The tempera paint conceals the joined edges well.

BOX PUPPETS

Single-serving cereal boxes from variety packs can be manipulated to serve as puppet mouths. The motion is similar to the moving mouth paper bag puppets.

ONE-BOX PUPPET

Cut through three sides of the box at the mid-point, and fold forward on the front to form the inside of the mouth. Put four fingers into the upper half of the box, the thumb into the lower half.

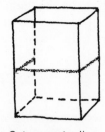 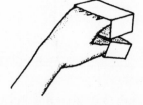

Cut on center lines.

TWO-BOX PUPPET

To represent a long-snouted animal, such as an alligator or wolf, two boxes can be used. Cut the top off each, and tape two long edges together. Manipulate just like the one-box puppet.

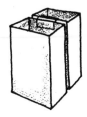

PAPER PLATE PUPPETS
(*Color Plate 11*)

BIG-MOUTH PUPPET

Fold the paper plate in half so it forms a huge grin. In order to open and close it easily, one of the following will be necessary:

· Paste half a paper plate over the top half to conceal the fingers, and a half plate or loop of tape on the bottom

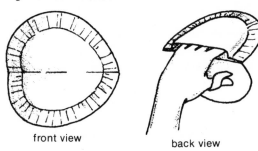

front view

back view

· Paste a piece of fabric over the top
· Paste the plate to an old sock; this will also conceal the arms of the puppeteer

Put the eyes and top of the head on the part of the plate that shows when the mouth is closed.

LITTLE-MOUTH PUPPET

1. Mark two paper plates lightly into sixths. (Measure the diameter; divide by two. Mark that distance off around the edge—it will fit exactly six times. Draw light lines connecting opposite marks.)

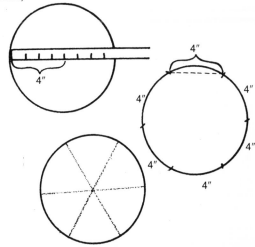

2. Glue the plates together, leaving two adjacent segments unglued.

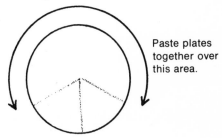

Paste plates together over this area.

3. Fold the upper and lower plates so the unglued segments separate to form a mouth as illustrated.

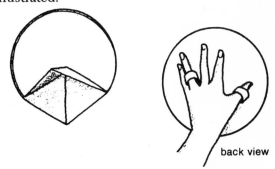

back view

4. Tape finger loops on the back for ease in manipulation.

MOVING EYES PUPPET

1. Draw circles for very large eyes. Make slits on both sides of circles leaving the tops and bottoms uncut.

2. Slide a narrow strip of posterboard or construction paper from the back through both eye openings. Draw the pupils.

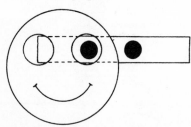

3. To make the eyes move, slide the strip back and forth, or jiggle it up and down.

MOVING TONGUE PUPPET

A moving tongue can be added to the moving eyes for an even more comic effect.

1. Slit the mouth, and insert a strip of red paper.

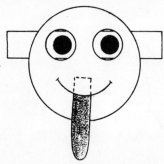

2. On back, use one paper fastener to attach the top of the tongue to the center of the eye strip. Insert another fastener from the front of the face (where it represents the nose) through the tongue strip. Now, when the eye strip pulls the pupils in one direction, the tongue moves in the opposite direction.

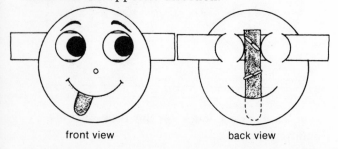

front view   back view

Children and teens with mechanical interests, even if they don't care to play with puppets, often take great delight in engineering coordinated movements. A cardboard box body can be added to the paper plate face so that arm and leg movements can be devised.

CARDBOARD TUBE PUPPETS
(Color Plate 11)

This is the quintessential clothed puppet and will serve as the model for puppet clothes-making.

NECESSITIES:
- A 3″ length of cardboard tube from inside foil or plastic wrap (If desired, paint it flesh color with tempera or acrylic.)
- Fabric at least 8″ x 14″
- Pencil
- Scissors
- Rubber band
- Paints and/or other decorative trims for face and clothing.

STEP-BY-STEP:

1. Trace the outline of the cardboard tube in the center of the wrong side of the fabric.

2. Cut slits from the center of the circle to the outline.

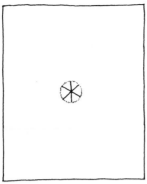

Clip as indicated.

3. Slip the tube into the hole from the right side so that all the little triangle tabs are inside. Secure the fabric to the tube with a rubber band.

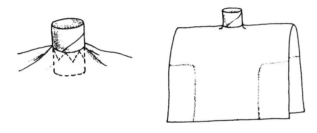

4. Fold the fabric in half, cut away rectangles on the sides, and stitch together all the cut edges except the bottom. (This can be done inside out on a sewing machine.)

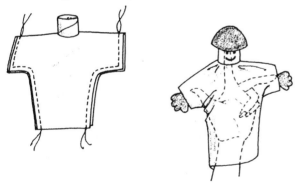

5. Draw a face, add a hat or yarn hair.

6. Trim the clothing with buttons, ribbons, etc. An optional addition would be felt hands at the end of the sleeves.

7. To manipulate the puppet, put the index finger into the cardboard tube, and the thumb and middle finger each in one sleeve.

ON YOUR OWN

• The part of the cardboard tube that extends above the clothing can be covered with a head made of papier-mâché pulp (see the next section).

• The cardboard tube can have a longer portion inserted into the fabric. The extra length can be slit and spread out to form "shoulders" to support the clothing.

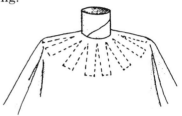

• For young children, felt is an excellent fabric to use because seams can be glued instead of sewn. Another advantage of felt is that it will adhere to itself temporarily without glue, so that an array of interchangeable clothing trims and accessories can be made from the scraps; each clothing variation can represent a different character. Felt rectangles come in many colors for just a few cents each in the 5&10.

• An alternative way to make the clothing allows the puppeteer's hand to go in through a slit in the back rather than from the bottom. This gives the option of finishing the bottom with full-length clothing and cardboard or papier-mâché feet when this will fill a need, e.g. for the story of Cinderella.

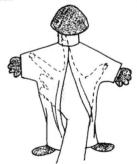

PAPIER-MÂCHÉ PUPPETS

Papier-mâché puppets are often preferred by older children. They are the most durable kind of puppet, and they can be given more detailed facial characterization than other kinds. They also require more ability from the puppeteer because there are no gimmicks like moving eyes or mouths to carry the burden of the action; the puppeteer must be able to move his fingers to give the illusion of whole body movements by the puppet. Children who are trying to perfect their technique will find it useful to practice before a mirror.

PULP PUPPETS
(*Color Plate 11*)

AGE: PRE-TEENS AND TEENS
TIME: HOURS, SPREAD OUT OVER SEV-
ERAL DAYS

If not acquainted with papier-mâché projects, read about papier-mâché pulp on pages 40–42. Each puppet head will require only a handful of pulp, so wait until there is a bit of pulp left over from a larger project and plan a whole family of puppet heads.

NECESSITIES:
· Papier-mâché pulp
· Cardboard tube
· Narrow-necked bottle
· Acrylic gesso
· Acrylic paints
· Acrylic matte varnish
· Fabric, construction paper, and optional trimmings for clothing

STEP-BY-STEP:
1. Form the papier-mâché pulp into a ball around a 3″ length of cardboard tube. One inch of the tube should be exposed below the puppet's neck.
2. Using fingers, model the facial features. The roughness of papier-mâché makes it particularly appropriate for witches, monsters, and grotesque characters. (Note, however, that papier-mâché

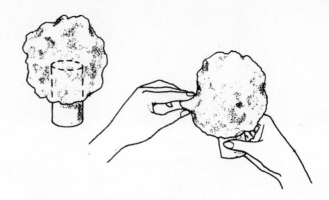

pulp can be smoothed with spackle when a fine-textured finish is wanted. For instructions, see page 48.)
3. Slip the cardboard tube onto a narrow-necked bottle and let it harden in a warm dry place for at least two days.

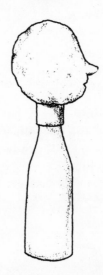

4. Seal the pulp with a coat of acrylic gesso. When dry, paint as desired with acrylic paints, and follow that with a final coat of acrylic matte varnish.
5. Make clothing as described under Cardboard Tube Puppets in the preceding section.
The illustrated witch has black yarn hair, a black fabric cloak, and a construction paper hat. The conical part of the hat is a rolled semi-circle. The brim is made and attached exactly like the brim of the papier-mâché fireman's hat, instructions for which are on page 49. For a richer black,

the construction paper was overpainted with black tempera.

ON YOUR OWN
• Papier-mâché puppets can also be made without the cardboard tube. In this case, model the pulp around two extended fingers, and make a flare below the neck to represent the shoulders and support the clothes. This puppet cannot slip into a piece of fabric like the cardboard tube puppet; it should be used when a more elaborate costume (such as a king's robe) is required, or for a smaller puppet's head than would be appropriate with a neck the size of a cardboard tube.

STRIP PUPPETS
The paper strip method of papier-mâché can also be used for puppet heads, but because they are so small, it is best to use shorter and narrower strips of paper than suggested in the instructions on pages 43–44. Suitable armatures are a rolled-up ball of newspaper taped to the end of a dowel, an old light bulb, or a plastic lemon.

ON YOUR OWN
• A puppet theater should be provided only after a child has expressed the need for it. A simple one can be made by cutting an opening in the bottom of a grocery carton, as illustrated. Later, when backdrops and scenery become important, a larger carton is needed with an opening on the bottom, through which the puppeteer can work, and a solid back which can accommodate interchangeable backdrops painted on kraft paper.

Rhythm Instruments * * * *

The importance of rhythm instruments for children is two-fold. First, rhythm is a basic element in everyone; second, it is the most basic and fundamental element of music.

For nine prenatal months the fetus is in continuous contact with the mother's heartbeat, and the rhythmic beat of a metronome often soothes fretful babies. The heartbeat is rhythm; breathing is rhythm; walking is rhythm. Nature is rhythm: the earth's rotation and revolution produce the cycles of day and night, and the yearly seasons.

In order for a child to understand rhythm, beginning with his or her own, we help him or her take it from within to where it can be seen. When a child can display rhythm either with the body (through dancing, running, jumping, etc.) or with an instrument (which is an extended part of the body), he or she can feel its essence and become more aware of it.

A good way to help a child feel rhythm is for an adult to tap the rhythm of a child's walking. Adapt the rhythm to the child's tempo; don't expect the child to change his tempo to an arbitrary rhythm at first.

Children enjoy keeping the rhythm of their own walking, running, or dancing. They also like to use rhythm instruments to accompany a pianist, or records, or their own singing.

As they become more discriminating, they can be encouraged to mark the rhythm of hopping, skipping, and other physical movements. Formal musical instruction frequently starts in just this way before the child is introduced to an instrument.

Historically, the first instruments were of the percussion type because it was rhythm that was the first element of music to be appreciated by primitive man. And so it is with children, whose individual development so often parallels the development of the whole human race.

A collection of rhythm instruments is a fine addition to the playroom; they will be used for many years. (It's a nice idea to select a color scheme in advance and follow it through with all the instruments.)

It is not necessary, or even desirable, to make all the instruments at one time. It is better to make them at intervals so that a child can have a chance to explore one thoroughly before being confronted with another.

The instruments are described in the approximate order in which children usually enjoy them, although there are of course no absolutes that must be adhered to. The age of the child will determine how much adult help is needed in making the instruments, but in nearly all cases, children can decorate them.

DRUMS

(Color Plate 11)

The child's first rhythm instrument is a drum, which can be used somewhere around the age of one, as soon as the baby's arms can make the swinging motion needed for banging. The simplest drum is made with a large can.

LARGE CAN DRUM

AGE: PRESCHOOL AND ELEMENTARY
      SCHOOL (WITH ADULT HELP)
TIME: MINUTES

NECESSITIES:
- Large can (such as from coffee or shortening) with plastic lid
- Extra plastic lid (optional)
- Cord, nail, and hammer (optional)
- Choice of decorating materials (yarn, paper, paint)

STEP-BY-STEP:

1. Wash and dry the empty can. The drum may have two plastic drum heads instead of one, if the bottom of the can is replaced with a spare plastic lid. The plastic has a gentler sound that may be preferable. But if one end is metal and one plastic, the child will become aware of tone differences.

2. If the child is to wear the drum around his or her neck, punch two holes in the can as indi-

cated, and tie a length of cord or yarn through them with the knot inside the can. For extra strength, braid or chain crochet the yarn. Adjust the length so that when the drum is worn around the child's neck, it will hang at waist level.

ON YOUR OWN
• For a child young enough to still be putting things in his mouth, an undecorated can is safest. For older children, see decorating suggestions below.
• To wrap large drum brush rubber cement around the can and wrap dip-dyed or other decorative paper around it, overlapping one inch and securing the overlap with rubber cement. To protect the paper against water and tearing, seal it with shellac or varnish, or wrap it with transparent self-adhesive contact paper.
• Wrap with potato-print paper (see page 59), dip-dyed paper (see page 126), or any other decorative paper.
• Decorate large can drum by wrapping with felt, fabric, or self-adhesive vinyl contact paper.
• Decorate large can drum by painting the can. Use acrylic gesso as a prime coat, and any other paint will adhere to that.
• To make more than one drum, use different sizes of cans. Encourage the child to discover the difference between the sound from a large can and a small can.
• A softer-sounding drum can be made from a round salt box or a round cereal box.

• If a coconut shell is cracked in half so that one of the halves is unbroken, stretch a piece of inner tubing across the opening and nail it all around the edges.
• Old kitchen gloves and an embroidery hoop can become a hand drum. When the fingers tear, slit one glove from the thumb to the cuff, and cut all the fingers off. (Save usable ones for finger puppets.) Stretch the flat part of the glove between embroidery hoops; 7″ diameter is about the maximum possible size. Cut away the excess. The tighter the glove is stretched between the hoops, the more resonant the sound will be.

YARN WRAPPED DRUM
(*Color Plate 11*)

AGE: PRESCHOOL AND ELEMENTARY
      SCHOOL (WITH HELP)
TIME: MINUTES

NECESSITIES:
· Can to be wrapped
· Nail and hammer
· Rug yarn (or alternative cord, twine, or yarn)
· White glue
· Brush and pan of water to rest it in

STEP-BY-STEP:
1. An adult should punch a hole close to the bottom of the can near the seam by hammering a nail into it.

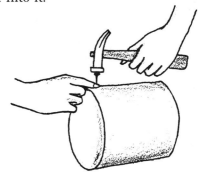

2. Insert yarn into the hole from the outside, and make a knot inside. Pull yarn from outside so the knot is tight against the hole. (Rug yarn is thick enough to make the wrapping go quickly,

but any other kind of yarn, twine, or raffia, can also be used.)

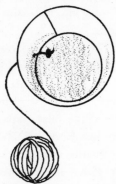

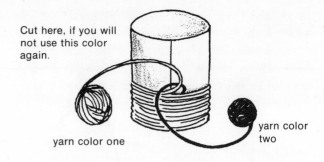

Cut here, if you will not use this color again.

yarn color one

yarn color two

3. *Starting the wrapping.* Brush white glue on the outside of the can from the bottom edge to about an inch up. Wrap yarn around the can, pressing it tight against the glue. If necessary, slide strands down so they lie close together and completely cover the surface of the can. When the wrapping reaches the top of the glue, brush glue on the next inch and continue wrapping.

4. Some people find it easier to wrap by holding the can still and winding the yarn around it. Others find it easier to hold the yarn and turn the can. Let the child use whichever method he or she starts with, but in case of difficulty, be ready to demonstrate the other method.

5. *Changing colors.* Always change colors at the seam of the can. About an inch before changing colors, lay the beginning strand of the new color along the seam line and continue wrapping the first color over the new color.

6. Make the color change just after the first color has passed the seam line. Lay the first color along the seam, and bring the second color over it and continue wrapping.

7. If the first color will be used again farther

up the can, it is not necessary to cut the yarn. Just carry it up under the other wrapping until it's time to change colors again.

8. If the first color will not be used again, cut the yarn so that an inch is left to lie on the seam to be covered by the second color.

9. *Ending the wrapping.* The easiest way is to cut the yarn an inch beyond where the wrapping ends, and tuck the excess under the last few rows of wrappings. (Work fast, before the glue hardens.)

10. An alternative method of ending is to punch a hole at the top, as at the lower edge, and pull the yarn through, making a knot close against the hole. This is a more secure method.

NOTE: Wrappings don't have to simply circle around and around. The yarn can be swirled in any kind of design. Just brush glue on one part of the can at a time. Do not punch a hole in the can to start the yarn; simply lay an inch or so of the yarn end where it will be covered by the first few swirls of yarn. At the end, push about an inch of yarn under the design. Do one color area at a time, and fill in the background last.

DRUMSTICKS
(*Color Plate 11*)

A double-headed drum beater is good for beginners around a year old because it assures that whichever end they bang with is the "right" end.

Cover each end of a dowel with a ball of papier-mâché pulp. (See page 40 for directions.)

A total length of 8–9″ gives a toddler better leverage than a longer stick.

The next day, after the outside is hard, slip the pulp off the stick so the inside can dry more quickly.

Papier-mâché pulp shrinks as it dries; when the balls are replaced on the dowel, there will be an empty space which must be filled with white glue.

Seal with acrylic gesso, paint with acrylic paint, and use a final coat of acrylic medium.

SPOON DRUMBEATER

Another kind of double-headed beater can be made with a wooden kitchen spoon. Leave the bowl on one end, and put a ball of papier-mâché pulp on the other end. Both ends are equally good for striking the drum, but each will slightly different sound.

Other things with which to beat a drum:
- Fingertips
- Knuckles
- The eraser end of a pencil
- Empty thread spools (make handles by pushing pencils into the holes)

RHYTHM STICKS

Take two wooden spoons and saw the bowls off the handles. Smooth the rough edges with sandpaper. The handles are used for rhythm sticks, which are played by tapping them against each other. Paint, if desired.

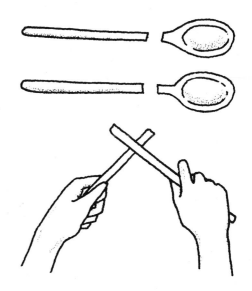

CASTANETS

The bowls of the wooden spoons will become castanets, which require more finger dexterity than little children yet have. Attach elastic or narrow ribbon across the center of the concave side of both bowls with contact cement or short tacks. Slip one over the thumb and the other over the index and/or middle finger, and click them together.

The spoon bowls can also be joined like traditional castanets, although they are much more difficult to play. Drill holes as illustrated

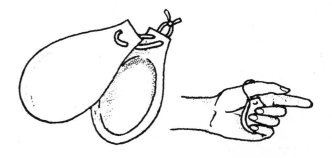

and knot a cord through them. Slip the cord over the thumb and click the spoon bowls together with the other fingers.

Castanets can also be made from walnut shells, following the same procedure as for the first spoon bowl castanets.

MARACAS
(*Color Plate 11*)

There are several ways of making maracas. They should all be tried because they all sound different, and because maracas are such a favorite that it's hard to have too many.

BALLOON MARACAS

AGE: PRESCHOOL AND UP (TO USE)
    ELEMENTARY SCHOOL (WITH HELP) AND UP (TO MAKE)
TIME: MINUTES, PLUS INTERVALS FOR DRYING

NECESSITIES:
- One or more small round balloons, preferably with long neck
- Dried beans or rice
- Funnel (optional)
- A handle. Suitable ones are:
  Handles from discarded utensils or paint-brushes
  A dowel between $\frac{3}{4}''$ and $1''$ in diameter
  Wood turnings from a hardware store or carpenter shop
- Masking tape
- Small empty can
- Papier-mâché strips and paste (see instructions on page 43)
- Spackle (optional)
- Acrylic gesso, paint, and medium

STEP-BY-STEP:

1. Put about a dozen dried beans into the balloon. A funnel makes it easy to pour them in.

2. Inflate the balloon to 4–5″ diameter. Knot it close to the inflated part, and slip the neck over the handle.

3. Use four strips of masking tape to hold the balloon straight on the handle. Wrap a fifth strip around the other four where they meet the handle.

4. Cover the entire balloon and masking tape with 6–8 layers of papier-mâché strips, following the same procedure as in covering the balloon for the fireman's hat, page 49. The handle may seem loose while the paper is still wet, but when dry, it will be rigid.

5. To dry the maraca, rest it in an empty can, handle upward, until the neck of the maraca is dry. Then reverse the maraca, putting the handle into the can, until the tip is dry.

6. If there are any very uneven areas, they may be filled in with spackle.

7. Seal with acrylic gesso, paint with acrylic paints, and finish with acrylic medium.

8. Maracas are played by shaking them rhythmically.

LIGHT BULB MARACAS

AGE: PRESCHOOL AND UP (TO USE)
    ELEMENTARY SCHOOL (WITH HELP) AND UP (TO MAKE)
TIME: MINUTES, PLUS INTERVALS FOR DRYING

These are easier to make than balloon maracas because the bulbs are firm and the handles are part of them. The sound is softer.

NECESSITIES:

· Burned-out electric light bulbs
· Small empty can
· Papier-mâché strips and paste (see instructions on page 43)
· Spackle (optional)
· Acrylic gesso, paint, and medium

STEP-BY-STEP:

1. The small size and extreme curvature of the light bulbs require narrower-than-usual strips of paper. Half-inch widths are most useful, but wider ones may be used crosswise on the handle, and narrower ones may be required in the concave areas.

2. Brush paste on the entire bulb before putting the first strips on.

3. Place the first strip from the base, across the top, and down on the opposite side to the base. Place the second strip perpendicular to the first, also from base to base across the top.

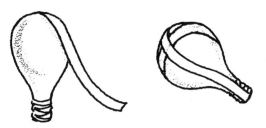

4. Place two more strips in the intervening spaces. Fill in the empty areas to complete the first layer of strips. Brush with paste.

5. Arrange the second layer of strips crosswise. Keep the strips short enough so they do not wrinkle on the curved parts of the bulb.

top view

6. Complete a total of six layers of papier-mâché strips.

7. To dry, stand the bulb with rounded end downward in an empty can. When the handle end is dry, reverse the bulb until the top is dry.

8. Give the maraca a quick rap against a hard surface, and the glass will shatter inside to provide the sound.

9. Follow steps 6, 7, and 8 under instructions for balloon maracas.

GOURD MARACAS

These are the easiest of all because gourds are sold at the market in the fall. Select shapes with handles, and use them for a table centerpiece for a few months. With luck, by midwinter the seeds within will have dried sufficiently to make a good sound when shaken. If not . . . well, they looked pretty anyway.

TAMBOURINE

(*Color Plate 11*)

AGE: PRESCHOOL (WITH HELP) AND ELEMENTARY SCHOOL
TIME: MINUTES

NECESSITIES:

· Two stiff paper plates, 6″ diameter
· A handful of dried beans
· Yarn and tapestry needle

- White glue
- Paint or pictures to paste on or other decoration

STEP-BY-STEP:

1. Hold both paper plates together and punch between 12 and 16 holes equidistant around the edge.

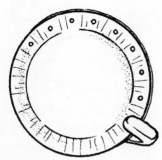

2. Hold the plates right sides facing, and put the beans between them.

3. Leaving a two-inch tail, wrap yarn through all the holes; after the last hole, wrap in the opposite direction. When the yarn ends meet, tie a knot and secure it with a dab of glue.

4. Paint or decorate as desired. To play, hold it in one hand and slap it against the palm of the other. Or, shake it.

ON YOUR OWN

- Use aluminum foil pie pans instead of paper plates.
- Instead of the beans (or in addition to them), jingle bells may be tied through the holes. Let the yarn ends hang loose.

Party idea! Birthday parties for preschoolers are never complete without a little marching parade. Before the party, make a tambourine for each guest, but do not decorate it. As each guest arrives, give him or her a tambourine and offer crayons, paints, or pictures and paste so each one can decorate a personal tambourine. The activity will keep the early arrivals occupied until everyone is there. After the party, of course, each guest takes home his or her tambourine as a party favor.

JINGLE CLOG

Loosely nail four metal caps from beer or soda bottles onto a flat-sided handle. Shake for a jingling sound.

SHAKERS

Different kinds of dried beans, seeds, and grains make different sounds in different containers. Experiment. Select one from Column A and one from Column B and see how many different kinds of sounds can be made.

A

Dried beans
Seeds
Rice
Unpopped corn

Small pasta shapes
Tapioca
Crushed egg shells

B

Metal spice cans

Plastic jars

Two paper cups, with
rims taped together

Two aluminum foil
tart pans taped
together

Two small cans (such
as for tomato paste
or frozen juice
concentrate) taped
together at the
open ends

A pull-tab soda can
(tape the opening
closed after inserting
the noisemakers)

Small boxes, as from
cereal variety packs,
or half-pint milk or
cream containers

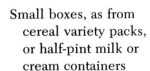

BELLS

Jingle bells are sold at the 5&10, mostly around Christmas time. They can be attached to:

· Handles, like the ones suggested for balloon maracas (see page 162)
· The wires of a pastry blender or wire whisk
· A bracelet made from the top of a styrofoam cup, or papier-mâché, or a circle of $\frac{1}{4}''$ wide elastic

GONG

An aluminum pizza pan makes an ideal gong. Drill a hole in the rim through which to tie a looped cord. (Just remove the cord to make pizza; the hole won't interfere.) Strike the pan with any of the beaters suggested for drums.

Can the child figure out why the gong must be held by the cord? How does it sound if the gong is held directly with the hand?

A pie or cake pan can be used instead of a pizza pan. Foil pans can be used, too, but they are not so resonant as the solid aluminum ones.

KAZOO

Halfway between a rhythm instrument and a melodic instrument is the kazoo, which can be used as soon as a child can hum a tune. Tape a piece of aluminum foil or wax paper part way around one end of a cardboard tube. Let it hang loose on bottom. As the child hums through the other end, the paper or foil vibrates to enrich the sound of the humming. The foil or paper may need to be adjusted, either closer to the tube or farther away in order to produce the most pleasing sounds.

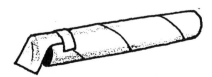

SAND BLOCKS

Glue fairly coarse sandpaper onto the large side of two metal spice cans. The kind of can with a small lid that fits into the top is better than the kind with a plastic lid which extends over the side. Rub the sandpaper sides against each other for a scraping sound.

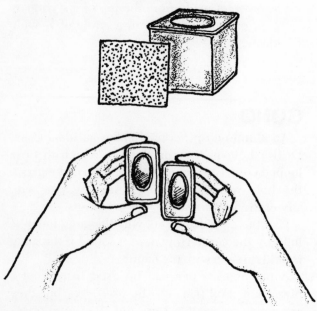

CYMBALS

Strike two pot covers together for a grand clashing finale to the music session!

Appendix--
A Guide to Recommended Products

In selecting materials to be used in projects, preference is given to those which can safely be used by children. A non-toxic finish that a child can apply is better than a toxic substance that should only be used by an adult, even though the toxic substance may give a more permanent finish. However, when the only suitable product is a toxic one, it will be recommended for use with the caution that that step be done by an adult.

In many cases, products are interchangeable. If there is a particular preference for a certain paint or varnish, either because of familiarity with its properties or because it happens to be on hand, by all means use it. If only one product is appropriate, the instructions will clearly state that fact.

There is also a conscious effort to limit the number of different products required. Preference is given to one product which can serve many uses, rather than a multiplicity of highly specialized products.

Adhesives

White glue is the generic name for such brands as Elmer's and Sobo, which come in plastic squeeze bottles with pointed tips. It has the widest number of uses and is the adhesive most frequently recommended in this book. Its advantages are:

- It is the strongest adhesive for porous items (paper, cardboard, fabric).
- It is one of the most permanent adhesives.
- It can be diluted with water and applied with a soft brush when a thinner coating is necessary.
- It is appropriate for all ages from elementary school upward, although a young child who is careful, or who is working on a protected surface with adult supervision, can probably use it.

It has only three minor disadvantages:

- Once it dries, it cannot be washed out of clothing or other fabrics.
- It causes colored tissue and crepe papers to bleed.
- It causes thin papers, including the above-mentioned, to wrinkle.

    (In some cases, bleeding and wrinkling may be a desirable element of the project; if not, use rubber cement.)

To apply white glue, always smooth the squeezed-out ribbon of glue with the fingertips (moistened, if necessary).

To speed up adhesion, let the glue become slightly tacky before pressing surfaces together.

White glues are also manufactured with different formulations to make them tackier or quicker-setting. Their trade names are usually variations of these descriptive qualities.

- School glue is one white glue variation, which is washable after it has dried; however, it does not have the same permanence as the regular white glue.
- White paste and library paste are generic names for a product sold in the 5&10, which is the only appropriate adhesive for pre-schoolers. You can make your own, following the recipe for papier-mâché thick paste on page 41.
- Rubber cement is a viscous adhesive which is used only for paper sticking because it prevents wrinkling. It is not permanent; if permanence is required, use contact cement. Rubber cement should not be used by children because the vapor is harmful; read the label cautions.

Specialized adhesives. For more difficult attachment problems there are specialized adhesives to be considered if white glue has not worked. Read labels carefully because many of them warn against use by children.

- Contact cement forms an instant bond without holding or clamping, but only after the cement has partly dried on the surfaces for 15 or more minutes. It is used primarily when one or both of the surfaces is a non-porous material, such as metal or plastic. It may also be used for papers when it is necessary to avoid the wrinkling of white glue and the impermanence of rubber cement. Because of label cautions, it should be used only by adults.

  At least two companies (Weldwood and Elmer's) have introduced a contact cement which is water-based and non-toxic and could be used by pre-teens. Be aware, however, that because it is water-based, it has the same wrinkling and bleeding characteristics as white glue. (Beware of another kind of instant-bonding adhesive which contains cyanoacrylate. The adhesive will actually bond skin together if handled care-

lessly; it is probably too risky to keep in a household where children can get at it.)

- Epoxy adhesive is a two-part compound which is mixed just before use. It forms the strongest and most permanent bond of all the adhesives recommended in this book. It is toxic and should be used only by adults and mature teen-agers.

NOTE: There are several acrylic mediums which are occasionally used as adhesives. They are described with all the acrylic products in the following section on paints.

Paints

Tempera paint is the only suitable paint for preschoolers, but is often used also by older children. Its main features are:

- It can be thinned with water, and it is washable even after it has dried (although some colors may leave staining).
- It comes in rich, thick colors.
- It dries to a smooth, opaque, matte finish.

Tempera comes in two forms: liquid and powder.

Liquid tempera is best to buy in one-pint plastic squeeze dispenser bottles. It is much more economical in large quantities than in the little jars from the 5&10, where one pays more for the jars than for the contents. A good school-quality tempera will stay usable for five years or more. If there is no art supply store nearby which sells it, ask at a local school for the name and address of the company from which they order school supplies. Most school supply companies will also send catalogs and fill orders for individuals.

Powdered tempera is mixed with water before using. It has these advantages:

- It costs far less than liquid tempera.
- It can be mixed to an extra-thick consistency so that beginners can paint without dripping.
- It can be mixed with a combination of acrylic medium and water to make a paint which is cheaper than acrylic but more permanent than tempera.

· It lasts indefinitely in its powdered form. Its disadvantages are:
  · The paint is not ready instantly. It takes a few minutes to mix, which may be bothersome when several colors are necessary.
  · Leftovers don't keep well. Black, in particular, turns moldy within a week.

Acrylic paints are more useful for more purposes than any other paints. Technically known as "acrylic polymer latex emulsion" paints, they are water-thinnable when wet, but permanently waterproof when dry. However, the dried paints are easily stripped from the hands and nonporous surfaces (Formica, plastics, metal) under warm water; once dry, though, they are impossible to remove from fabric and from paint brushes. For this reason, acrylic paints are generally reserved for children over age eight. But with proper precautions and supervision, you may be willing to let your younger child use them.

Acrylic paints come in two forms:
· Jar paints, usually sold in hobby and craft stores, have the consistency of sour cream and dry to an opaque matte finish. They are the best for most craft projects.
· Tube paints, usually sold in art supply stores, have a toothpaste consistency and dry to a semi-gloss finish. For most crafts projects they must be thinned either with matte medium to reduce the gloss, or with gloss medium to enhance it. Water may also be added, but not more than the amount of medium; otherwise the binding quality of the paint will be too greatly reduced.

If you have acrylic tube paints on hand from painting canvases, by all means use them. But if you are buying new paints for crafts use, select jars. Avoid those that come in prepacked sets of six jars; they are generally of poor quality and too thin to provide good coverage.

Acrylic paints are part of a whole family of acrylic products.

Mediums contain the same polymer binders as the pigments; they are used to thin the paints without reducing their adhesion. There are two kinds of medium:
· Gloss medium adds a high luster to the pigment. In addition to thinning, it has two other uses:
   As a varnish over acrylic paints when a high luster is desired.
   As a glue in tissue collage (see instructions for Tissue Collage Egg, page 118).
· Matte medium reduces the luster of the pigment. In some brands matte medium is also used as a varnish; in other brands matte medium and matte varnish are two separate products.

Acrylic gesso is a white painting ground which can be used as a primer on any surface (even plastic and metal) and can be covered with any kind of paint. It is a most useful undercoating when you want to conceal the color of the original item (e.g., papier-mâché, cardboard, and cartons).

Acrylic gel is an extra-thick gloss medium which is used in several projects as an adhesive that will partially embed three-dimensional objects such as seeds and beans.

Acrylic modeling paste is a mortar-like substance which is used in several projects for embedding mosaics and seeds.

Felt-tip markers (wide tips) and **fiber-tip pens** (fine points) come in two forms:
· With washable ink, suitable for all ages
· With permanent waterproof ink, suitable for those over age eight

They are useful where it is necessary to have firm control of the color in a small area (see Pseudo-Pysanky Eggs, page 123).

Model airplane paints are glossy enamels suitable for those over age eight. Their main advantages are:
· They come in tiny jars at a very low price,

so that a full range of colors for small work can be purchased quite inexpensively.

· The metallic gold, silver, and copper are extremely beautiful and useful paints.

Their main disadvantage is:

· Cleanup requires turpentine or paint thinner, which are best restricted to teens and older.

Oil paints are not recommended in this book because they have largely been superseded by acrylics, which dry faster and are easier to clean up. There is only one project in which oil paints are essential: Marbleized Eggs (page 121).

Finishes

Finishes protect painted surfaces from dust and deterioration. Some of them can also be used as undercoatings to seal a surface before painting.

Acrylic varnishes are preferred whenever possible because they are non-toxic and can be used by those from age eight upward. They *must* be used over:

· Permanent felt-tip markers and fiber-tip pens. (Any other finish will cause those permanent inks to bleed.)

They *must not* be used over:

· Water-soluble paints, such as washable felt-tip markers and tempera paints. (It makes those paints run.)

They *may* be used over all other paints.

Acrylic varnishes are available in both glossy and matte finishes.

Shellac and **varnish** are to some extent interchangeable. The main differences are:

· Shellac is cheaper and faster-drying
· Varnish is more durable and slower-drying

The following is a more detailed comparison to help you in choosing:

	Shellac	Varnish*
Drying time for one coat	30 minutes	3 hours
Drying time for recoating	2–3 hours	Overnight
Solvent, thinner, and brush cleaner	Denatured alcohol	Turpentine or paint thinner or mineral spirits
Resistant to water	No	Yes
Resistant to alcohol	No	Yes
Suitable for outdoor use	No	Yes
Can be used as sealer *under*	All paints except felt-tip markers and fiber-tip pens	All paints except *permanent* felt-tip markers and fiber-tip pens
Can be used as finish *over*	All paints except *permanent* felt-tip markers and fiber-tip pens	All paints except *permanent* felt-tip markers and fiber-tip pens
Age range	Teens and adults	Teens and adults
Color	Almost clear	Amber cast
Consistency	Thin	Heavy

° There are several kinds of varnish. The synthetics known as "polyurethane varnishes" are extremely strong and are the ones referred to in this book when not otherwise identified.

Epoxy resin finish is a permanent, plastic protective finish consisting of two parts, a resin and a hardener, which must be mixed in equal parts just before applying. In this book it is recommended for craft items that are used outdoors or that require washing. It is sold in craft shops as a one-coat epoxy finish for découpage. It is essentially the same as the clear epoxy paint sold in hobby shops for finishing model airplanes. Some of these products have their own brand-name solvent/thinner, but ordinary lacquer thinner works as well. Epoxy finishes all have harmful fumes; some are also flammable. Their use should be restricted to adults and mature teen-agers.

Polyester resin (also known as casting resin) is a crystal clear plastic to which a few drops of hardener are added before use. It can be brushed on like the epoxy finish, or poured into a mold. Its main advantage over epoxy varnish is that it is colorless and therefore better over white paint. All other finishes have more or less of an amber cast. Like epoxy, polyester resin has toxic fumes and should be used only by adults and mature teenagers.

Clear nail polish can be used over most paints; it has a glossy finish. It has these advantages:
· It comes in small bottles.
· It is readily available everywhere.
· It can be used by children as young as eight.
· Its built-in brush eliminates the need for brush cleaning.
Its disadvantages are:
· It cannot be used over model airplane paints (they would bleed).
· It can only be used on small projects.

Clear plastic sprays are used only when there is no other alternative because they have too many disadvantages:
· They cover so sparingly that they require many coats in order to build up a protective surface.
· They are far more expensive than comparable non-spray products.

· Because of toxic fumes their use is restricted to adults and mature teen-agers.
· Because of spray drift, a paint shield must be set up around the object to be sprayed.

There has been much publicity recently about the dangerous effects of aerosol sprays on the earth's protective layer of ozone which shields us from harmful ultra-violet rays. This, however, is *not* among the disadvantages of clear plastic sprays. The propellant implicated in the ozone depletion theory is fluorocarbon, which is used primarily for personal care products (hair sprays, deodorants). The propellant used for paints, varnishes, and most household cleansers is hydrocarbon, which is not at the present time suspected of environmental damage.

Brushes

The right brush for each job can make the project easier to do and better looking. Buy the best quality brush available; one good brush will outlast two cheaper ones and will give better results.

These are some ways to prolong the life of brushes:
· Do not leave brushes standing on their bristles. Suspend them so the bristles are in an appropriate liquid (the paint itself, or its solvent), but without touching the bottom of the container.

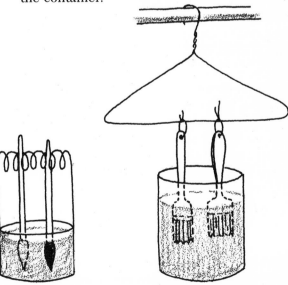

- Clean and wash brushes immediately after use.
- Keep brushes separated according to the solvent in which they are cleaned. Brushes which are cleaned with water should not be interchanged with those cleaned with alcohol or turpentine.

These are the brushes most useful for craft projects:

Nylon brushes are always used for acrylic paints. They may also be used for tempera paints when a smooth finish is important. Useful sizes are:
- Flat brushes 2″, 1″, ½″, and ¼″ wide. (The wider ones are better buys in hardware stores; the narrower ones will probably have to be bought at an art supply store or a craft shop.)
- One or two small, round-pointed brushes.

Black bristle brushes are used for tempera, primarily by children. They are much cheaper and coarser than the nylon brushes and can withstand the scrubbing action that beginners tend to use. Good widths are 1″ and ¾″; small children should be encouraged to paint freely, with large strokes.

Soft brushes (e.g. camel hair or squirrel hair) are useful for thin paints, airplane enamels, and diluted glue when smoothness is essential. Practical sizes are ½″ flat, and one or two small round ones which come to a fine point.

Varnish or glue brushes have coarser bristles and are necessary because the products are so thick that they might pull more delicate hairs out of the metal ferrule. Large size varnish brushes must be bought at a hardware or paint store. Small ones come in packages of six in hobby shops; they are so inexpensive that many people discard them, rather than cleaning them, after using epoxy or polyester resin finishes.

Brush substitutes are sometimes useful:
- Cotton swabs or toothpicks can be used for small touch-ups, or when it's too much bother to clean a brush.
- Kitchen sponges can be cut to any size and fitted into a spring clothespin handle. These are good brushes when a large quantity are needed for a group of children, or to provide a separate brush for each of many paint colors, when an inexpensive wide brush is needed, or simply as an economy measure for small children.

- A strip of cardboard or the plastic tab from a bread loaf wrapper can be used to apply a thin smooth layer of contact cement.

Solvents

Solvents are used to thin paints and finishes and to clean brushes (and fingers, if necessary). The solvents required for projects in this book are as follows:
- Denatured alcohol, for shellac
- Turpentine, for airplane enamels, oil paints, and polyurethane varnish
- Paint thinner and mineral spirits, odorless, and equally effective, substitutes for turpentine
- Lacquer thinner, for epoxy resin, polyester resin, and contact cement

Tools

Needles are used for stitchery and weaving. They vary in eye size and kind of tip. Select a needle with a large enough eye to thread the yarn easily. Select a blunt or sharp tip depending on the fabric to be penetrated.
- Tapestry needles have a large eye and a blunt tip. They are used for weaving and needlepoint, and they may be used for stitchery on canvas or loose-woven fabric. They range

from #13 (the largest size, for use with rug yarn) to #22 (the smallest, for fine yarns and embroidery floss). Buy them in yarn shops.

- Embroidery or crewel needles have a long eye and a sharp point. They are used with fine yarns, crewel wool, and embroidery floss on tight-woven fabrics and non-woven fabrics (felt). They range in size from #3 (the largest) to #9 (the smallest). Buy them wherever sewing supplies are sold.
- Chenille needles combine the large eye of the tapestry needle with the sharp point of the embroidery needle, and are used with thick yarns on tight-woven or non-woven fabrics. Their numbers correspond with tapestry needles. Buy them wherever sewing supplies are sold.

Craft and utility knives make neater and more accurate cuts than scissors, particularly on cardboard and styrofoam. They consist of two parts: a handle and replaceable blades. X-Acto is a trade name for knives sold in hobby stores, which are narrow-handled and come with an assortment of blades. Hardware stores carry thick-handled utility knives with replaceable razor-like blades. Look for such safety features as the self-storing retractable blades featured on the Stanley knives, and the automatic blade guard on the Lewis Safety Knives. But with or without safety features, craft and utility knives are only for use by adults and mature teen-agers.

Index to Projects